Once Upon a White Man

A memoir of
War and Peace in Africa

by
Graham Atkins

First published 2008
Reprinted August 2014
Perth, Australia

To Kyle and Chelsea – a reminder of your roots

And to Michael (Mhaka)

Acknowledgements:

My father Roderick (Tommy) (now deceased), and my aunt Zoma, provided valuable background information about my grandfather.

Thanks to Jenny de Lange and Jenny Balson for reading and providing comment on the early drafts.

Special thanks to my family for their moral support and encouragement during the writing of this book.

Front cover photo – by Avryl Atkins

Contents

MAP of ZIMBABWE (formerly Rhodesia)

➤ Route of Pioneer Column (1890)

X Historic Battle Site

0   100   200   300 KM

N

Prologue

Once you have lived in Africa, so all the old hands tell us, you can never get it out of your system. I too have come to realise this is true. Perhaps it simply has to do with the astounding beauty and diversity of the land, the sheer intensity of the experiences it offers, or the pulse of the ancient rhythms that rise from tribal drums and seem to echo through its very soul. Even the air in Africa seems to absorb the vibrancy of life and the intensity of sudden death in a way that makes every gulp taste vital and full.

Or perhaps it has something to do with an instinctive connection we have with a continent that is modern man's original home. DNA research shows that every human on earth is linked back to a common African mother, a prehistoric "Eve" who once walked the gorges of the great African Rift Valley over two hundred thousand years ago. So when even the most hardened traveller is awed by Africa's forests, mountains and waterfalls, or when we relish a sunset churned dust-red by elephants, perhaps what we feel is more than just appreciation for nature, perhaps it is indeed an instinctive tug from our past, a deep visceral connection with our ancient roots.

This is the story of my own deep ties with a continent that retains its power, allure and mystery even today.

- Book One -

Rhodesia

1 Now and Then

My ambush is set. The late evening rays of the lowering sun stab through the bushes and dance a jig across the killing ground in front of me. Birds, now familiar with my motionless body, swizzle and chirp carelessly in the nearby bushes. Beneath my face I smell the warm mustiness of the soil. Inches away, ants scurry to and fro, searching for food. While I wait to dispense death, life is busily recycling itself all around me...

When you lay an ambush, your first priority is to select a suitable killing ground. You must choose a spot where you know your enemy will have to pass. Look at a documentary film showing rebels laying an ambush for a government patrol, and you will see what I mean. The ambushers invariably select high ground overlooking a road or track. The road is hemmed in on both sides by steep slopes, and from the vantage point of the attackers there is a clear line of fire. On the open ground below, there will be no cover for those caught in the ambush – nowhere to hide, nowhere to run. They don't call it a killing ground for nothing.

When you set your ambush, your next consideration is concealment. You will need to work hard on your personal camouflage, pulling branches and twigs around your head and shoulders, smearing zig-zags of black camouflage cream on your face and arms to break up your silhouette, and hiding the glint of your binoculars behind dark coloured netting. Part of the trick is not to conceal yourself in an obvious spot - behind a lone bush for example

- for when your enemy fires back, they will target such obvious cover.

 You can initiate your ambush with rifle fire, but a better method, if you have enough time beforehand to set it up, is to use something with greater hitting power, such as a claymore mine. Triggered by an electrical circuit, a claymore will send a lethal arc of lead shrapnel across the killing ground, delivering an early knock-out blow and reducing the risk of a counter-attack.

 All things considered, an ambush is a nasty, one-sided piece of work...

 I am still lying beneath the bushes. It feels like hours have passed. The furnace-red sun kisses the horizon and a hot bead of sweat trickles across my eyebrow. I feel my camo' paint start to run, but I resist a worsening urge to scratch my nose. This endless waiting is always the hardest part...

 Then the birds stop singing.

 I tense. My thumb gently flicks off the safety catch of my rifle. I blink the sweat from my eyes, and focus down the sights. My finger curls around the trigger and I hold my breath.

 There's a soft, distant crack of a twig. Then a slow shadow slips and ripples across the yellow grass. From my concealed position, I watch as a furtive shape moves in front of me. It morphs into a single, silent figure. It's a young woman. The enemy comes in all shapes and sizes - sometimes you're not even sure if it isn't just some civilian who's wandered into the wrong place. But there is no doubting the intent of this one. Her approach is cautious, calculating. Her steps, as careful and light as a cat, probe the ground ahead for more crackling twigs that will betray her approach. Her eyes flick from side to side, probing every likely hiding place, searching for me in the lengthening shadows. In a last ray of sunlight, I see the glint of her AK-47 rifle; the red-brown of its wooden butt is polished the colour of blood.

She halts, tensed, her instincts picking up danger. I allow myself the faintest of smiles. She will never see me, not until it's too late. I inch the barrel of my rifle a little higher, squinting down the sights until I can draw a bead on her chest.

A familiar tingle crawls at the back of my neck. Blood begins to throb in my temples. *Mur-der, mur-der,* it chants, an insistent, beating echo from the past. I try to block it out, but the taunt continues. *Mur-der, mur-der...*

Suddenly there is a whispering in the air behind me. Something dark and metallic thuds into the shadows next to me. My heart stutters, races, my throat constricts. Even before I look, I know it's a grenade. Damn!...

"BOOM! You're dead, dad!" Kyle shouts excitedly, leaping out of his hiding place.

"Yes, yes, I know."

"Then die, die!"

"Okay, okay." I roll over, clutching my chest dramatically, obediently coughing my last, trying to still my racing heart.

My daughter, Chelsea, saved from her own imminent execution on the killing ground, races up, pumping additional rounds into my expired form and into her brother for good measure. "Got you, got you both!" she hollers.

I lie on the ground in a pool of blood. "You guys are getting too good at this," I complain. "Some old soldier taught you too well."

"You did, dad." They both laugh and dance around me, high on adrenalin. My kids always get a great kick from playing this game, even though some might consider it not very PC.

After a long while, when my heart has stopped pounding in my ears and my arms are no longer shaky, I stand up, dusting bits of grass and leaves from my shorts. I glance at my watch. "Time to get ready for bed, kids."

"Aaw, do we have to?"

"Come on, guys, you know it's school tomorrow." Domestic stuff. Here and now.

My kids grab my hands, one each side, and we head for the house. They scuttle off to brush their teeth, chattering expansively to each other, well pleased with the outcome of their game. I take a deep breath, forcing the last faint chants of my muttering demons back into their dark box, then follow my children indoors.

Chelsea is ready for bed first. "Tell me a story, dad. Please. You tell good stories." I don't, but she always tries to flatter me. She can wrap me round her little finger by turning on the charm.

Kyle is also listening now, hovering at the bedroom door, wary of breaking into the father-daughter time, but keen not to miss out on anything special. He too chips in.

"Yeah dad, tell us one of your stories. It's good to tell your kids about the olden days."

"Not that old," I protest.

"Tell us about the time you threw a brick through the policeman's window," prompts Chelsea. "Tell us about that."

"I didn't throw the brick, Chelsea," I say.

"Yeah, but you drove the getaway car!"

"No, I just happened to be *in* the getaway car. There's a difference, you know."

"Or tell us about when you stole the train."

The kids aren't giving up now. They're both suddenly animated at the prospect of hearing an old story retold, or perhaps even becoming privy to a new one. "Tell us, dad, tell us!" they shout excitedly, urging me on. If it's a story that involves their own childhood, that's even better. For, in a way, they too, long to be re-connected with their roots.

I lie back on the pillow and close my eyes. The past, which is always crouched there, waiting, rumbling like an old dog, springs suddenly into focus. Everything jumps haphazardly inside my brain – once again I can smell the dust, can hear the thumping beat of village drums, can see the waving crimson leaves of the *msasa* trees.

My children are watching me, waiting, expectant. I look into their eager faces. There is so much to tell. I want them to remember the same things that I remember, to share the passion I have for Africa's beauty, its sounds and rhythms, its smells and colour, its anything-goes sense of freedom. For it is their heritage too.

But – I rub my hand over my eyes – some of it is difficult to recount; the greed, the insults, the lost opportunities. And the violence and the killing - that's the hardest part to tell. The sound of gunfire and green tracer in the night and the pants-wetting sheer terror of knowing you could die at any minute. The curse of a voice in the darkness – "You British, go home!"

I don't know if I will be able to tell them everything.

I glance at the clock. "Alright," I grumble. The kids sigh with anticipation, and stretch out on the bed. Now even the fading photos on the bedroom wall seem suddenly to have pricked up their ears, waiting expectantly, as if they too might be lifted from their own suspended animation, be cleansed and forgiven by the simple act of recounting the past.

So I go back - back, into the shadows, transported to that other world, that previous life, as if I am wrapped in my own version of a time machine...

2   Words of Warning

When I was six years old, the arm-rest of my grandfather's rocking chair was my favourite perch. Seated there in the cool shade of his veranda, I could keep an eye on what games my cousins were playing, but at the same time was able to enjoy the company of the leathery old man of whom I had grown so fond. Grandad and I would discuss anything that came to mind. Sometimes it was the story about the imaginary exploits of the porcelain pirate that sat on a perch above his rattan-weave chair. Sometimes, if I was lucky, he would talk about 'the good old days', telling me stories about his adventures in the African bush – tales of ox-wagons and big-game hunters, of the Zeederburg coach that was pulled by teams of zebras, or he would recount old yarns about his attempts at prospecting for gold. But mostly we talked about everyday things – how many rabbits or turkeys he had in the sheds, about his daschund Mitzi and her latest litter of puppies, the state of his vegetable garden, or what I had been doing at school during the week.

Grandad was retired. We kids often stayed the whole weekend on his rambling smallholding. We played with our Dinky cars in the garden, making small rivers with dripping water from the garden taps and building roads and bridges for our toys. When we tired of this, we would raid the vegetable gardens for carrots, beans and granadillas, or explore the maze of old storerooms that dotted the garden. Grandad's earlier passion for gold prospecting always meant his storerooms were littered with fascinating kit from the old days, and we delighted in rummaging through his obsolete mining equipment, swinging hook-shaped picks and poring over old prospecting licences.

Perhaps my first suspicion that disturbing winds of change were beginning to blow came one day as I sat with him watching the Shona labourers in the vegetable garden. The men, as usual, were hard at work, digging. They always sang as they wielded their hoes – a vibrating, rhythmic chant that seemed to turn their back-breaking labour into a kind of slow-motion war-dance. The songs carried clearly, the chants lifting and whirling into the shimmering summer heat like musical dust-devils.

"Didn't you say you once found gold, Grandad?"

For a while the old patriarch didn't reply, which was unusual. Grandad was always chatty. As the silence stretched into minutes, I turned back to watch the men in the fields.

"You need lots of luck to find gold," Grandad replied suddenly. Then he added thoughtfully, "You need even more luck to hold onto it." He paused. "I reckon I had just enough luck to keep me out of trouble."

"What sort of trouble?"

Again, there was no immediate answer. The old man was gazing into the distance, as if he was remembering something from long ago.

"Like when you shot those snakes?" I prodded. I remembered the story he'd told of how he'd stumbled across two black mambas while out hunting, and how he had managed to kill both of them with a single shotgun blast as they reared up to strike.

Grandad's leathery eyelids widened as the memory came back. He chuckled. "Yes, I guess that was one time when I used up quite a bit of my luck, alright." Then he turned to me, suddenly serious. "You know, lad, I have had to face snakes and lions and madmen, and at the end of it all, I never got rich. But I've been able to live in this country without much worry. And there's the end of it. Soon my days will be over, and the past won't matter to me one way or another. But..." He paused, and gazed out over the waving fields of beans and carrots, as if unsure how to carry on. "Do you know who Cecil Rhodes was, lad?"

"Of course, Grandad. He was the founder of our country. Rhodesia was named after him."

"That's true, of course," replied my grandfather. "Rhodes was a luckier man than me. He found gold – lots of it. But that was nothing compared to what he could do when he put his mind to something. Did you know that Rhodes single-handedly stopped the Matabele rebellion? Yep, if he put his mind to it, that man could do anything."

Grandad paused, fiddling with his pen-knife, then he pulled a chunk of dried biltong from his pocket and cut us both some pieces. We chewed on the spiced meat.

"I'll tell you something, lad. What Rhodes could do really well, better than any other white man, was get the Africans and Europeans to work together. The Africans really respected him, you know. When he died, they were the ones who allowed his body to be buried at World's View at Matopos. That's one of the most sacred places of the Matabele, so it shows just what they thought of him." Then he sighed deeply. I wondered why he suddenly seemed so sad.

"Something happened to Rhodes," he continued. "I don't know what it was, whether he lost interest in this country, or if he had other things on his mind, but somehow, before he had finished building bridges between blacks and whites, he stopped. What I mean is, he didn't finish the job. Not properly. Not so that Africans and Europeans were really ready to live together."

I looked at my grandfather. His eyes, it seemed, were far away. I wondered why he was telling me this. Did he expect me to answer? Then impulsively the old man put his huge sun-burnt leathery hands on my shoulders and looked me full in the face. In a voice low and tinged with regret, as if I, a child, were the only person he dared confide his fears to, he whispered, "I think, now, there's a bit more trouble around the corner in this country than most folks care to talk about."

I looked past my grandfather's wrinkled face and rheumy eyes, over his shoulder to the spray of golden droplets flung into the air by the twirling irrigation sprinklers. I noticed the singing of the Shona men in the lands had stopped. All I could now hear was the metallic *clank-clunk* of the old borehole pump as it struggled to suck up enough water to keep the delicate English vegetables alive in the dry African sand. A breeze had picked up out of nowhere, and it teased the dampness of my shirt. I felt suddenly cold, as if a shadow had fallen across me, blotting out the warm sun. I shivered.

3   Voices from the Past

My grandfather's veiled warning did not mean much to me at the time, partly because I was so young, but also, I now realise, because I had little knowledge of the history of southern Africa and the fortuitous, perhaps inexorable chain of events that had led to me being who and where I was as a white child in Rhodesia in 1964…

The indigenous inhabitants of central and southern Africa and perhaps the people who have been closest to the ancient soul of the continent, are the Khoi-San, a race of small, yellow-skinned hunter-gatherers. The San had lived in harmony with nature for tens of thousands of years, but around a thousand years ago, they found themselves displaced by a massive tide of Bantu migration from the north. The black-skinned newcomers are believed to have originated from Nigeria, West Africa from where they had migrated in search of new pastoral lands and places to settle.
Around the same time as the Bantu migration reached southern Africa, Arab traders were sailing their dhows down the coast of Africa in search of gold, copper, ivory and slaves. The trade winds that carried the Arabs on their journey reached as far south as Mozambique, and from here the Arabs were able to penetrate the heartland of Zimbabwe. Under their king Monomotapa, Zimbabwe's Bantu people forged strong trading ties with the Arabs which gave rise to the building of the impressive stone city, Great Zimbabwe.
By the 14th or 15th Century, however, the Zimbabwe civilisation went into decline – the enigmatic Zimbabwe

bird sculptures fell from their plinths, and the stone city at Great Zimbabwe was abandoned. The remnant Bantu tribes dispersed over the countryside, reduced once more to a purely subsistence existence, and the mists of time once again hid Zimbabwe from the world.

Four hundred years passed, and then, around 1835, events suddenly broke over the region with a vengeance. It came in the form of a fierce dark wave of warriors who suddenly appeared on the horizon. This was the "Amandebele", or Matabele as they came to be known, the "people of the long shields". The Matabele were an offshoot from the warlike Zulu nation. Not so much a tribe as a standing army, the Matabele had spent the past two decades plundering their way through the top end of South Africa and Botswana. Now they were in search of a new neighbourhood in which to live. Mzilikazi, their ruthless leader, surveyed the peaceful lands of the now defunct Monomotapa Empire, and nodded with approval. The area had two big advantages – excellent grazing for his cattle, and easy access for rape-and-pillage raids against the terrified local Mashona. It looked the perfect spot to call home.

By 1498, Portuguese explorers had opened up the southern sea route to India, and European ships were routinely plying back and forth around the Cape of Good Hope. As they rounded the treacherous southern tip of Africa, the Dark Continent to the north held no attraction for these Europeans – they labelled the continent's interior "terra incognita", and filled in the gaps on their maps with pictures of dragons and savage beasts. It was not until 1652 that the Dutch, under Jan van Riebeeck, established a permanent victualing settlement at Cape Town. They were pleasantly surprised to find that the Cape colony, with an agreeable Mediterranean climate, proved capable of supporting all the requirements of European agriculture – wheat, fruit and vegetables, vineyards and European domestic animals.

After the annexing of the Cape Colony by the British in 1805, and the granting of equal rights to "free persons of colour" in 1828, many resident Dutch farmers decided to leave the Cape. The 'Boers', as they were known, trekked east and north in search of new farmlands. However, in the vicinity of the Fish River they collided with the southward migration of the Xhosa Bantu and a number of skirmishes took place between the two groups. It was the precursor to a racial and economic conflict that would span the next two hundred years.

In the 1860's, diamonds and gold were discovered on the highveld of South Africa. News filtered back to the Cape Colony and to Europe, spawning a rush of excited prospectors into the interior. Over the next few years, many men made their fortunes on South Africa's new diamond and gold fields. Few, however, did as well as one new immigrant – Cecil John Rhodes. Rhodes – he of "so much to do, so little time" fame – was an energetic entrepreneur with a shrewd eye for business and a knack for getting on the right side of people. In less than twenty years, he made himself a fortune and, for good measure, became Prime Minister of the Cape Colony. Rhodes, however, had an even greater ambition: to expand the reach of the British Empire across Africa and pave the way for his personal dream, the building of a trans-African railway from Cape to Cairo. Rhodes knew that the only practical route to Cairo was northwards across territory that belonged to the fierce Matabele. Rhodes was no fool – he recognised that a fight with the Matabele was not the best way to get what he wanted, and sensing that negotiation was a better, and cheaper, option, he dispatched his representative, Charles Rudd, to the royal kraal at Bulawayo.

By this time, Bulawayo was awash with hunters, miners and government envoys, all bombarding the new Matabele king, Lobengula, with requests for mining concessions, treaties and exploration rights. Rudd, however, soon got the ear of the king when he revealed the deal Rhodes had in mind in exchange for mining rights – the offer included money, a thousand Martini-Henry rifles, and a steamboat on the Zambezi River. Initially Lobengula was undecided, but finally the lure of the rifles proved too much and he signed Rudd's concession.

It is unlikely that Lobengula, illiterate and dependent on translation, understood the full import of the wide and ambiguous terms that he signed that day. In part, Rudd's concession reads: *"I, Lobengula, King of the Matabele... do hereby grant ...the said grantees... the complete and exclusive charge over all metals and minerals situated and contained in my kingdom...together with full power to do all things that they may deem necessary to win and procure the same..."* It is doubtful that such a powerful monarch, who had once defeated the Boers on the battlefield, would have willingly ceded control of his country to such a degree if he had known the true extent of Rhodes' colonial ambitions. Rudd, of course, would have had every reason not to reveal more than necessary to the king. But once the concession was sealed, such debate was academic. As far as Rhodes was concerned, the way was now legally clear for him to launch his greatest venture.

Rhodes' plan was to send a "Pioneer Column", under the auspices of his chartered British South Africa Company, through the land of the Matabele and, once clear of danger, to grab as much territory in Mashonaland and beyond as possible. The column was hastily assembled.

When ready, it comprised over a hundred wagons, nearly 200 pioneer settlers, 500 BSA Police, and a thousand bearers and labourers. They were equipped with horses, field guns, Maxim and Gatling guns, searchlights, and rifles. In June 1890, the pioneers departed from Mafeking, crossed the Shashi River and entered Matabeleland. Their arrival, of course, did not go unnoticed. To the Matabele, the column looked more like an army of occupation than a mining venture, and the Matabele *indunas* urged Lobengula to defend his kingdom. The king, however, was hesitant. After all, he had given permission to the white men to dig for gold, and the intruders, though well armed, did not appear to pose an immediate threat. (In fact, the pioneers had deliberately picked a southerly route through the lowveld which avoided coming anywhere near Bulawayo for that very reason.) As the pioneers pressed on, hacking their way through the thickly wooded lowveld, Lobengula continued to hold back his eager warriors.

After a few weeks, the pioneers left the lowveld and emerged onto open grasslands, where they established Fort Victoria. Relieved that the crossing of Matabeleland had gone without incident, the column then proceeded unhindered into Mashonaland. After a few more weeks, they reached their assigned destination, a boggy piece of ground near a small rocky hill. On the 13th September 1890, they raised the Union Jack, declared the land for the Empire, and named the site Salisbury.

The arrival of the pioneers at Fort Salisbury signified to Rhodes and his supporters the founding of a new country that was soon to become known as Rhodesia. The eager pioneers spread out and began to peg their farms, dig for gold, and generally lay claim to the land. The local Mashona people simply looked on with a mixture of concern and bemusement.

Although there had been little trouble getting to Mashonaland, it was clear to Rhodes and others that the Matabele still posed a threat: after all, Lobengula had granted the settlers mining rights, but the king still regarded Mashonaland as his personal domain and the Mashona as his lowliest subjects. Tensions inevitably rose. The new Administrator, Leander Starr Jameson, who had been appointed by Rhodes, was clearly of the view that the troublesome Matabele needed to be sorted out once and for all. Jameson readied a column of armed men, and waited for a suitable pretext. When it came, in the form of reports that some of his troopers had been fired on near Fort Victoria, Jameson sent a despatch to Rhodes noting *"We have the excuse for a row... and the getting of Matabeleland."*

Jameson's punitive column headed towards Bulawayo, and soon encountered a large *impi* of Matabele near the Shangani River. The Matabele attacked. Against the withering fire of the settlers' Maxim guns, however, they had little chance. They suffered huge losses and were forced to withdraw.

The two forces clashed again at the Bembezi River. Once more, the Maxim guns inflicted terrible damage on the Matabele warriors, who fell by the thousand. By the end of this second encounter, the back of the once famed Matabele army had been broken.

Jameson's column now proceeded unhindered to Bulawayo, but Lobengula had already given the order to burn everything and had fled into the bush. Jameson knew that the Matabele war would not be over if the king was still free to rally his people, so he sent out a reconnaissance patrol under the command of Major Allan Wilson. Wilson crossed the Shangani River and against orders, pushed on through the night. At dawn, the patrol stumbled across the encamped Matabele, and came under attack. Wilson retreated, but the Shangani had risen in flood overnight, and his escape route was cut off. Wilson now had no choice but to stand and fight. Against thousands of charging Matabele, Wilson and his men held out as long as they could, but there was no hope of rescue or escape. Wilson and his 16 men died fighting.

But Lobengula was also nearing his end. With the soldiers still on his tail, the king fled north. When he reached the Zambezi River, he called a halt. Despairing at the situation which had overtaken himself and his people, Lobengula decided to end it all - he took poison and died. His body was taken by his followers to a nearby cave, placed inside, and the entrance sealed and hidden, forever.

Over the next few years the defeated Matabele sulked and brooded. With their land taken by the Europeans, their warriors forced to grovel as menial labourers, and the bulk of their cattle either confiscated or dead from *rinderpest*, the once mighty Matabele now looked to their spirit mediums, the *ngangas*, for help and guidance. In early 1896, as if on cue, the moon went through an eclipse. The *ngangas* could not have asked for a more auspicious sign, and they instructed their warriors to launch a new attack on the white men.

The 1896 Matabele uprising was sudden and ferocious. The Matabele took to the countryside wielding assegais and rifles (rifles supplied a few years earlier by Rhodes). They looted stores and homesteads, and hacked to death without mercy any whites they caught out in the open. The settlers responded by rushing their women and children into fortified *laagers* in the main towns, and sending out armed patrols to intercept the marauding Matabele. However, the Matabele had learnt the folly of frontal attacks during the war against Jameson three years earlier, and now they pursued a successful guerrilla campaign. Even when extra troops were rushed in from the Cape, the authorities were unable to restore order.

Then, as if things weren't going badly enough for the settlers, the unthinkable happened – the previously docile Mashona, inspired by the example of the Matabele, joined the revolt. Their first victim was a Lomagundi miner whose body they tossed down his own mineshaft. Within days, the Mashonaland countryside was ablaze: groups of natives roamed the *veld* looting and murdering, and the surviving settlers fled for their lives to the safety of the Salisbury *laager*. In an uncanny parallel with the political crisis they would face exactly eighty years later, everything the whites had built up now seemed at stake: the country was in flames, there was no business being conducted, and no white man could move without an armed escort.

Always a practical man, Rhodes realised that a military solution to the crisis in Matabeleland would be unthinkably expensive, both in lives and money. Rhodes now became a convert for peace. Against the advice of those who wanted to prosecute the war to the bitter end, Rhodes, taking a few close aides, and unarmed, entered the Matabele stronghold in the Matopos Hills, and sought out the Matabele *indunas* to discuss an end to hostilities. At the Great Indaba that followed, peace was brokered. It seemed to everyone that finally the new country of Rhodesia had a bright future ahead of it.

4   In Search of Gold

Born into a large family of eleven children, my grandfather, Leonard Frank Atkins grew up in the small south-east English town of Bruton. His father was a simple horse and cart man, so the family teetered on the edge of poverty. Small wonder, therefore, that the young Frank, once tales reached him of opportunity and riches in South Africa, quickly decided that the colonies offered better prospects. So, obtaining passage as a carpenter on a wooden ship, Frank set off in search of his future.

The journey to Africa was not without risk – ships of the day foundered on a regular basis in the wild Atlantic seas that pounded the Skeleton Coast. Frank's luck held, however, and after several weeks he was rewarded with one of Africa's most iconic sights – the view of Table Mountain rising steeply from the sea. After the gentle, domesticated landscape that he had left behind in England, the sight of the sheer grey mountain topped by a white tablecloth of cloud must surely have been an unforgettable sign to Frank that he had arrived in a powerful, strange and enigmatic new world.

Disembarking at Cape Town and following in the footsteps of countless others who had come to seek their fortunes, Frank made his way inland. Eventually he reached Johannesburg, the fabled City of Gold. But he was too late - the easy pickings of the gold-rush were over and the mines were now the domain of powerful corporations. Frank decided to push on to Pietersburg in search of better prospects. Once there, to make ends meet, he took piece-work as a carpenter and a painter.

Frank, however, was sorely disappointed. His dreams of making a fortune had evaporated and he seemed no better off now than he had been in England. What should he do? Then one day he fell into conversation with some travellers recently returned from up north. The travellers told Frank how Cecil Rhodes had negotiated an end to the Matabele Rebellion and that, blessed with peace, rich agricultural soils and a perfect climate, Rhodesia was now a country of unparalleled opportunity. There were also rumours, they said, of many undiscovered deposits of gold in the hills. Compared to the disappointments of South Africa, it all sounded wonderful to Frank's ears, and he immediately made up his mind to head north. With barely more than the clothes he stood up in, a battered hat to shield his eyes from the glare of the sun, and a gun to shoot food for the pot, Frank mounted a bicycle and pedalled north as fast as he could to see what a future in Rhodesia would bring.

When he reached Mashonaland, Frank immediately set about searching for gold. With a prospecting pick at his side, he spent the next few months clambering over promising-looking granite outcrops. The views from these *kopjes* would have been impressive – untouched woodlands stretching endlessly into the distance, with an occasional rocky *kopje* bursting through the trees like a grey whale breaching a sea of green. Along the edges of grassy *vleis*, animals such as eland, zebra and elephant fed, while overhead eagles soared and cumulonimbus clouds towered. Frank, however, had no eyes for the view. His attention was focused on chipping away at the reluctant granite, desperately searching for the quartz veins that would, with luck, reveal the nugget of his dreams.

My grandad, Frank Atkins, with his wife, May, and children Roderick (my father) and Zoma (my aunt)

Grandad on one of his hunting trips

Left: Aunt Zoma
Above: Grandad's house and
smallholding at Hatfield, Salisbury

Meikles Hotel in central Salisbury, circa 1971

After weeks of continuous frustration in the hills, Frank retreated to the shady banks of the rivers that criss-crossed the countryside. There, with only a native servant and an occasional passing prospector for company, he spent months panning the river sands looking for gold washed down in the previous rainy season. Panning was perhaps more depressing than working the *kopjes* – after swilling away the sand, there were always tantalising traces of gold in the pan, flecks of yellow enough to make the heart soar – but always it was just a trace – too little to justify the effort, but just enough to convince him to struggle on.

My grandfather's dream of finding a pot of gold slowly faded. Love, however, blossomed. Frank met a bubbly young girl, Edith May Roberts, whose Irish parents had migrated from Kilkenny. After a suitable period of courtship, Frank proposed, and together Frank and May established a garage and trading store in the small village of Hartley. Frank taught May to drive a car, and she subsequently became the first woman to be issued a driving licence in Rhodesia.

Behind their garage, in a cottage with a wide wooden veranda, the couple raised two children: my father, Roderick, and my aunt Zoma. This was the first generation of our family to be born outside Europe. Growing up under wide sunny skies, Roderick and Zoma sunk their roots deep into the rich red earth of Africa.

5   Foundations

Unlike its *apartheid* neighbour South Africa, early Rhodesia had a meritocracy as its political system - the right to vote was determined, not by race, but by one's level of education and ownership of property. By the 1960's only a small number of Rhodesia's blacks actually qualified for the vote, but the reality was that the black electorate was growing fast enough that their numbers could be expected to politically overwhelm the white electorate within twenty years. When white Rhodesians realised this – their greatest fear was to be ruled by a black majority - their conservative nature came to the fore and they began to campaign against the existing constitution.

On the other end of the political spectrum, African nationalists, encouraged by independence movements elsewhere in Africa, were demanding more rapid progress towards majority rule. Tensions inevitably began to grow between the races.

In 1962 elections were called. The African nationalists, flexing their newly-found muscles, began to fan unrest in the native townships. Riots flared, and police and dogs had to be called in to restore order. On voting day, high levels of intimidation kept a crucial number of black voters away from the polls.

This proved to be a pivotal moment for the nation. If enough black voters had cast their votes that day for the incumbent United Federal Party, the moderate Prime Minister, Edgar Whitehead, might have retained power and a gradual and peaceful transition to majority rule may have been negotiated. As it was, however, the absence of moderate black voters allowed the conservative Rhodesian Front party to secure a narrow but crucial majority.

With Rhodesia now in the hands of conservative forces, the scene was set for the country to slip into a worsening clash. On the one side, frustrated by racism and impatient to gain political power, were the growing forces of black nationalism; on the other side was an increasingly obdurate white settler government which insisted that it was far too early to consider majority rule, that a government run by blacks would not be capable of maintaining "civilised" standards and would reduce the nation to a basket case "like the rest of Africa".

By 1964, Ian Douglas Smith, a celebrated World War 2 pilot, had taken the helm as Rhodesia's Prime Minister. When he took his oath of office, Smith could have had little idea that he was about to preside over the beginning of the most turbulent period in his nation's history.

6   Night Raid

I woke to the sounds of car doors slamming and raised voices outside my bedroom window. Someone was shouting in Shona, and another voice, unmistakeably European, cursed. A light was flashing insistently through the gap in my bedroom curtains, splashing the room with repetitive bursts of blue. I glanced at my bed-side clock. It was three a.m.

I threw off my bedcovers and padded across to the window. A soft warm October breeze ruffled the curtains. Peering through the window, I saw the grey bulk of a van parked in the driveway. A blue emergency light twirled round and round on its roof. I could make out a uniformed man standing next to the van, shining a torch up and down our driveway. What, I wondered, were the police doing in our garden?

As I watched, a stooped figure stumbled out of the darkness into the torchlight. Instinctively he raised a hand to shield his eyes from the glare, but not before I caught sight of a face contorted with fear. A second policeman, a black constable, prodded the hunched figure forwards with his truncheon. When the two figures reached the rear door of the police van, the captive appeared to resist. For a moment his hand grabbed the side of the vehicle.

"*Mompara!* Idiot!" The constable brought his truncheon crunching down on the offending wrist. There was a stifled cry, but with his grip lost, the captive was bundled into the van and the metal door slammed shut.

"One, *chete*," called out the constable.

"Okay," replied the officer with the torch.

Then I watched as the officer turned to face the house. "Sorry for the disturbance, sir," he said, his clipped English tones unmistakeable. "We won't need to trouble you again." I suddenly realised the policeman was addressing my father, whom I hadn't noticed, standing, half-concealed, in the shadows near the house. The officer, without waiting for a response, eased himself into the driver's seat of the police van and started the engine. The vehicle reversed out the driveway, granite chips crunching beneath the wheels. Once out the gate, the driver gunned the engine and the red tail lights of the police car disappeared down the dark street.

In the silence that followed, I gave a quiet cough to announce my presence. "What's going on, dad?"

My father's face turned towards me. "Oh, you're up, are you? Don't worry, son, it's nothing."

"Why were the police here?"

"Er... it was just one of the cook's girlfriends. You know, black women, *umfazis*, aren't allowed in white areas at night."

"It didn't look like a girl," I objected.

"That's enough questions, son. Now get back into bed." My father's voice had turned uncharacteristically abrupt.

I climbed back into bed, and the sounds of the African night rolled back in, once again cloaking the house in a host of comforting chirps and hoots. Telling myself everything was okay, I closed my eyes and tried to sleep. But in the darkness, strange images of witchdoctors and *tokoloshes*, spirits, seemed to be dancing above my head in time to flashes of blue light, and I tossed and turned restlessly until dawn.

7   Chatter

The image of the man being bundled into the police van kept returning to haunt me. Nobody mentioned it the next day, and even when I enquired of Daiton, our gardener, he was unusually evasive. "Ah, *picannin* boss," Daiton replied, sporting his trademark smile, "Sometimes the police they come to check, *shupa shupa*, all the time, but *mina aikona asi.*"

Even Daiton's pidgin English was too great a language barrier for me. Town kids didn't learn African languages – that's just they way it was. I suspected, however, that there were things going on outside my narrow, cocooned existence of which I knew almost nothing.

Accordingly, I resolved to pay more attention to what was happening in the world of adults. I began to loiter at the fringe of my parents' tea parties and sundowner sessions, trying to tune in to the conversations going on. Men and women invariably kept apart at these social gatherings, the men congregating with beers around the billiard table or *braai*, the women sitting in the lounge having tea. As I skirted the edge of my mother's gathering, listening for clues, I found the conversation among the women was focused almost entirely on the misdemeanours of their respective domestic staff. Comment swung from the mundane – "They really can't clean anything without breaking it" – to the, frankly, bizarre – "The cook thought when I said "get rid of the cat", that I meant I wanted it killed. So, can you believe it, next day I found it dead in the rubbish bin!"

I had more success near the billiard table – the men seemed much more forthright about political events, "The Situation" as they called it. As I listened to snatches of conversation, I heard about things that had never been part of my world before.

"This trouble in the townships. These bloody *kaffirs* are getting more and more cheeky by the day," muttered one sun-weathered individual.

"This is what happens when you educate *munts*," replied another. "They start stirring up the others."

"As for the blerry British government," opined a third, "they just don't seem to get it. If we give in to these demands for majority rule, this place will become like the rest of Africa in no time flat." A volley of nods followed.

The longer I hung around the adults, the more I realised that an undercurrent of tension pervaded everything. I heard whispered references to the rape of nuns in the Congo, and the murder of white farmers in Kenya. The men put on a show of bravado whenever the subject came up, but the women seemed to become more nervous, twittering anxiously amongst themselves, china tea-cups balanced on their knees, and casting worried glances in the direction of their men folk, as if seeking reassurance that there was no cause for alarm.

8   Winds of Change

Since the early 1960's, a number of Britain's former colonies had been granted independence. However, Britain's non-negotiable pre-condition for granting white-controlled Rhodesia its own independence was that black and white Rhodesians should have equal voting rights regardless of education or other measure i.e. one-person-one-vote.

The reaction from my parents' generation varied from indignation to outright hostility.

"Majority rule, hey? Easy for them to say," muttered my father, "they won't have to live with the mess."

No-one in my parents' circle disagreed. To do so would have been committing social suicide.

One day, I found myself standing at the school urinal. The gleeful shouts of children playing *stingers* in the playground drifted in through the breezeblocks above my head. A lizard scuttled across a bright patch of sun, chasing a fly. Suddenly a shadow loomed over me. Out of the corner of my eye I could see two grazed knees, and a pair of scuffed brown leather shoes. A boy, several years older than me, was standing there.

"What do you think people should vote?" the boy asked, out of the blue. His tone suggested that he held strong views on the subject, and that there was only one correct answer.

I only vaguely knew what he was alluding to – I had heard my parents mention something about our Prime Minister, Ian Smith, asking white Rhodesians if they wanted independence from Britain. I had no idea what independence meant, nor even how to spell the word.

"I'm not sure," I answered, stalling for time. I wished fervently that someone would appear and rescue me from this obvious bully. Avoiding eye contact, I concentrated on trying not to piss on my new shoes.

"I want a proper answer from you," demanded the boy.

What should I say? Panic overwhelmed me. Then a name popped into my head. "Harold Wilson," I blurted out. "He's crazy!" I had a vague notion that British prime ministers were generally considered to be the bad guys.

"'Harold Wilson' Now there's public enemy number one." The boy grinned at me as if I had suddenly become his best buddy. Evidently I had passed some sort of test. "We'll show Harold Bloody Wilson and those Brits that we can't be pushed around, hey?"

Clearly this was a good time to say as little as possible. I nodded agreement enthusiastically.

"My old man says we should definitely vote 'Yes' for independence," continued the boy.

"Oh. Oh, yes, my dad says the same," I volunteered weakly. There was an uncomfortable pause, neither of us knowing what to say next.

"My dad shot a *munt* on our farm last year," the boy unexpectedly proffered, as if this was somehow relevant. From his tone he might as easily have been discussing the shooting of a rabbit. "For stealing *mealies*," he continued. "My dad says *munts* will steal anything. He says it's in their culture." Over the coming years I was to learn that unquestioning acceptance of our fathers' actions and political views was a defining characteristic of a "good" Rhodesian.

"Mmm," I replied, non-committal. These abrupt statements were really starting to unnerve me and I was scared of saying the wrong thing. I wished this conversation was over.

"Right, I gotta go," said the boy suddenly. "See you later." He vanished as abruptly as he had come, leaving me alone to contemplate my narrow escape and my wet shoes.

9   Independence

In 1965, as events moved inevitably towards a political showdown between Britain and Rhodesia, Ian Smith's cabinet retired behind closed doors to consider their options.

Then someone announced, "The Prime Minister is on the radio!" We rushed to listen, holding our collective breath. It was the 11th November. Ian Smith's distinctive voice on the radio was firm and unfaltering:

"...We, the Government of Rhodesia, in humble submission to Almighty God who controls the destinies of nations.... and seeking to promote the common good so that the dignity and freedom of all men may be assured, do, by this proclamation, adopt enact and give to the people of Rhodesia the constitution annexed hereto; God Save The Queen."

Timed to remind Britain of our contribution in two World Wars, Smith announced that, rather than submit to Britain's prescription for majority rule, his government would seek an alternative political future. Rhodesia would now "go it alone". This was our UDI, a Unilateral Declaration of Independence.

In reality, it was a blind jump into the unknown.

10 Rice Pudding

Immediately after the UDI announcement, our biggest worry was that Britain would send in troops to reinstate the Queen's authority over rebel Rhodesia.

To our surprise, however, no British troops appeared on the horizon to put down our little rebellion. Weeks passed into months and with no sign of an invading force, we started to relax. The most obvious battle seemed to be the one for our hearts and minds: the government implemented stringent censorship of all news reports and soon my father's morning newspaper was peppered with small white spaces where the censors deemed the information likely to cause "alarm and despondency" among the community. (Leaving blank spaces in the newspaper was quickly added to the growing list of subversive activities that were prohibited by law.)

To punish us for UDI, however, the United Nations imposed international sanctions. "Listen to this," said my father, reading his morning copy of the Rhodesia Herald. "The United Nations Security Council has declared Rhodesia *'a threat to world peace'*. Can you believe it? What a joke! I bet most people in the world have never even heard of Rhodesia before now! And can someone please tell me exactly what sort of threat we are, and to whom?"

The British sent frigates to the Mozambique channel to blockade incoming oil shipments. Soon imported luxury goods – Clarkes shoes, Shredded Wheat cereal, Cadbury chocolates, and a hundred other things – vanished from our stores. Heartened by the thought that our rebellion would crumble if we didn't have Kelloggs for breakfast, Harold Wilson confidently predicted Rhodesia's economic collapse *"in a matter of weeks, not months"*.

But the mood in Rhodesia was defiant. Local entrepreneurs rushed to manufacture substitutes to fill the supermarket shelves, and with South Africa supplying a crucial lifeline of petrol, the economy soon rebounded. Farmers diversified their crops from tobacco to wheat, cotton and fruit, and new factories sprang up, producing shoes, clothing, furniture, groceries, wine, batteries, fridges, TV's, boats, truck bodies, tyres, fertiliser and chemicals. If the quality of local products was sometimes questionable (the early Rhodesian wines, for example, tasted like vinegar, and were certainly more dangerous), patriotic locals were generously forgiving "in the national interest".

Coming, as they did, out of the Depression and two World Wars, austerity was familiar territory for my parent's generation. Hoarding and recycling was now refined to a new art form: newspaper, milk bottle tops and glass were all assiduously collected for recycling. At home, our cupboards filled with empty tins, buttons, old fabric, nails, pipes, lengths of wood, and a wide array of other bits.

"What will we do with all this stuff, mum?" I asked.

"It'll all come in useful one day," she answered. "Now, help me find a place to store these jam jars."

Apart from a shortage of my favourite breakfast cereals, to me as a kid not much seemed to change after UDI. In fact, the only blemish on my childish horizon was rice pudding.

Rice pudding was dad's favourite dessert, and mum dutifully served it every Friday lunch. My brother and I would stare at the bowls of ghastly white stodge swimming in warm milk, and blanche. Dad meanwhile would be wolfing his pudding down, smacking his lips loudly, and declaring "Lovely, dear" with irritating gusto. After dad had finished his lunch, Mum would begin to clear the table, while Martin and I continued to stare morosely at our rice puddings, as if willing them to disappear. I always refused to eat mine. My brother, however, would sometimes put a blob of strawberry jam onto each separate grain of rice, then attempt to swallow the grains one by one. It drove mum to distraction.

By two o'clock, mum usually gave up waiting. "You're not leaving this table until you've finished your food," she would declare with finality. Then she would stride out the front door and start furiously digging in her garden.

This was the moment my brother and I had been waiting for. We grabbed our pudding bowls, dashed to the back of the house, and lobbed our congealed lumps of boiled rice, strawberry jam and sour milk over the hedge into the neighbour's garden. Then, terrified our treachery would be discovered, we sprinted back to the dinner table. Arriving back undetected, we made a suitable clatter with our spoons in the empty bowls, and shouted out together at the tops of our voices, "Finished!"

11 Stop the Enemy Coming In

In 1966, a small band of insurgents crossed the Zambezi from neighbouring Zambia and murdered a white farmer. Rhodesians were shaken by the sudden evidence that "our" Africans were prepared to take up arms against their white masters. The government rushed to allay our fears. The "terrorists" were, we were assured, just a few misguided "garden boys", a rag-tag bunch of malcontents whom the communists had brain-washed and sent into battle as part of a Cold War attack against Christianity and western civilisation.

Between 1966 and 1972, several other armed incursions took place. Each time the army dealt quickly and effectively with the insurgents who, we were confidently assured by our commanders, were no match for our army which they touted as the "best counter-insurgency force in the world".

December 1972, however, signalled a change of fortunes. Altena farm, a small homestead in a rich farming district north of Salisbury, was attacked at night by terrorists firing AK-47's and rocket propelled grenades. The attack only caused minor injuries to the occupants of Altena, but the incident was soon followed by attacks on other farms. Over the next few weeks, two farmers died and twenty soldiers were killed or injured in "follow-up" operations. The Prime Minister appeared on TV, grave, referring to "a new problem on a new front", but also reassuring the nation that everything was under control.

Control, however, was a luxury Rhodesian forces were not going to see much of again. The terrorists had learned not to repeat the errors of the past. They no longer fought pitched battles with the army, preferring instead to strike at soft civilian targets, then melting away into the dark. Their other strategy was to infiltrate the Tribal Trust Lands, living off the local Africans while indoctrinating them politically. The guerrillas forced the peasants to attend *pungwes*, propaganda sessions, where they were made to sing liberation songs and listen to grand promises of a future African paradise after the "*marungus*" had finally been driven from their land. Villagers who failed to show enough enthusiasm at the *pungwes* were beaten as a warning to others to support the revolution. Those suspected of being "sell-outs" or informers were often tortured or killed.

By 1973, a classic guerrilla war was under way. While the authorities railed at the "cowardly communist terrorists" who refused to stand and fight, the reality was that the tactics that the insurgents had now adopted were perfect for a campaign which aimed to tie down government troops, damage civilian morale and stall the economy. In their efforts to make the country ungovernable, the insurgents also had time and world opinion, on their side.

Now when we drove to Inyanga for our holidays, we carried a loaded shotgun in the car. As my parents chatted in the front seat, I was allowed the exciting privilege of pointing the shotgun out the back window. As I felt the cold metal of the breech in my hand, I itched for an opportunity to pull the trigger and see what damage a gun could do.

A song came over on the car radio, interrupting my parents' conversation. "Hey, listen, it's Clem Tholet," said my brother. The popular tune crackled thinly...

"For we're all Rho-desians
And we'll fight through thick and thin

We'll keep our land a free land
Stop the enemy coming in..."

We all joined in the singing loudly. Outside the cocoon of the car, the yellow grass blurred past...

"We'll keep them north of the Zambezi
Till that river's running dry
And this mighty land will prosper
For Rhodesians never die..."

Occasionally a lonely farmstead appeared through the *msasa* trees, wrapped tightly behind security fencing and barbed wire.

"The farmers out here have Agric-Alert radios," explained my father. "If they get attacked by terrorists, they can call up other farmers in the area, and a reaction team is sent to help."

"And they've got grenade screens on their bedroom windows, and tunnels to escape down," chimed in my brother.

To me, a city boy, the heady rush of a real life game of cowboys and Indians sounded much more exciting than my own boring suburban existence. Squaring off against terrorists, defending your farm, had all the glamour of Good standing up against Evil. Everyone knew how brave our farmers were, defenders of all we stood for, and our front-line against the communists. What I didn't yet know was the grim reality of life on the farms – bitter, worried men locking their families behind security gates each sunset, loosing their dogs, then waiting out the long nights behind sandbagged windows and grenade screens, nerves peeled for the sound of strangers beyond the fence. I couldn't begin to imagine the desperation in a father's voice when he was forced to call over the Agric-Alert "We are under fire", and heard the reply "Try to hold them off, John, we'll be with you in forty minutes."

After a tiring drive up to the cottage at Inyanga, mum tucked us into our cosy beds and blew out the paraffin lamp. As her footsteps receded, my brother's voice piped up from the darkness, "There's a terrorist under your bed."

"Is not," I protested. But I checked anyway.

12 In the Eye of the Beholder

"Our blacks", Ian Smith told us confidently, "are the happiest in the world". Cocooned in middle-class comfort, and more than keen to hold on to our privileged lifestyle, most whites were happy to believe whatever good old Smithy told us. Convinced by the anecdotal evidence all around us that Africans were naturally inept and prone to drunkenness and thieving, there was little desire to question too closely whether or not the civilised society and standards that we were so proud of extended to ensuring an equal and fair go for everyone.

"But they earn so little," a visitor from Europe would argue after learning our servants earned just $8 a month.

"Ah, but compared to most of Africa, they are really very lucky. They have jobs, a roof over their heads, extra rations, and they get treated well."

"But they have so many children to feed."

"Exactly. If they stopped breeding like rabbits, they might find it easier to make ends meet. It's population growth that's the real problem in Rhodesia."

In some respects that was true; hamstrung by international sanctions, yet facing one of the highest population growth rates in the world, the problems of black poverty, disease and unemployment seemed intractable to most white Rhodesians. Growing up with these issues as a constant backdrop to our lives, most of us had learned that to empathise too deeply with the plight of our fellow countrymen was to risk being emotionally sucked dry. Most of us, therefore, simply closed our minds and got on with our own insular lives.

13 School Days

"C'mon, Atkins," urged Jake Morton, leaning out the window of his battered Morris Minor. "Why don't you join us for a toot?" I was usually regarded by the cool kids at school as a bit of a nerdy outsider, so the uncustomary invitation to join them had significant appeal. On the other hand, underage drinking was a serious breach of school rules, not to mention that, as a prefect, I was supposed to uphold those rules.

"What about our school uniforms?" I asked. Our purple blazers were a bright beacon that could be easily spotted by Mr Jardine, the Deputy Head.

"Don't worry. We'll sort that out. Get in."

Still not entirely convinced this was a good idea, I nevertheless climbed into the back of Morton's car, squeezing between Brent Westgate and another boy, and we roared off down Jameson Avenue. A few minutes later we pulled up outside the Park Lane motel, and clambered out.

"Turn your blazer inside out," instructed Morton.

"What?"

"Inside out. Jardine will never spot us then." Unused to such subterfuge, I did as I was told, my blazer instantly transformed from a day-glo purple to a nondescript dull grey. Thus attired, we entered the beer-garden and settled in.

The afternoon passed in an increasing blur of drinking, rude jokes, and mini-soccer. Unused to alcohol, I found myself staggering about and making as much noise as the others. Outside, the evening sky slowly turned from blood red to dark purple. Our stomachs began to rumble.

"Let's get some graze," Westgate suggested.

"Good idea." We climbed back into the Morris Minor. I was feeling suspiciously nauseous, but didn't want to look like a *woos* by pulling out of the adventure at this stage. We headed for the nearby Gremlin drive-in restaurant. As we rounded a corner near our destination, the car tyres squealed and our weak headlights caught something on the road ahead. It was an African cyclist. He wobbled erratically in the beam of the headlights. "Fucking pissed *kaffir*," cursed Moreton. He yanked angrily at the wheel and brought the car slewing across the front of the cyclist, cutting him off and forcing the hapless African and his bicycle into the ditch.

"Hey, hey, check that *munt* go down!"

Morton brought the car to a slithering halt. He leapt out, and stormed back towards the African who, swaying on his feet, was contemplating his bent bicycle. The two other boys followed Morton. Naively, I thought they were going to help. Then, as I peered with beery eyes through the misted-up rear window, I was shocked to realise they were attacking the cyclist. With two swings of his fists, the stocky Morton brought the drunk African crumpling to the ground. "Sorry, baas, sorry," I heard the African cry. Moreton swung his boot into the man's ribs, and the black gasped. Then, as he lay there winded, Westgate bent down and smashed a fist into his face.

Headlights suddenly swept across the scene, and another car approached. I hadn't moved, so stunned was I at the shocking scene that had played itself out so abruptly before me. Ignoring the passing car, Morton directed one last blow at the inert African, then stood up, straightening his shirt. He said something to the other boys, and the three of them swaggered back to the car.

"Bloody *houts*," Moreton said, breathing heavily as he clambered back behind the wheel, "we should cull the lot of them,"

"Bloody bastards," Westgate agreed.

Shocked by what I had seen and disgusted with my inaction as much as by what the others had done, I didn't say a word.

14 A War of Words

As the war against the terrorists worsened through the mid-seventies and the casualties rose, the government found it was easier to rally white Rhodesians against the common threat of terrorism than it had ever been to get them to agree on other areas of national policy. State controlled TV and radio bristled with rage at the horrific acts of the terrorists – the rape of women, the abduction of children, the hacking off of limbs and burning alive of innocent civilians. The government propaganda machine lost no opportunity to remind us that most of these atrocities were committed by blacks against their own people.

There were a few dissenting voices: Allan Savory, a National Parks ranger, turned politician, urged his fellow whites to see the civil war as a cul-de-sac. "Without a change of heart," Savory thundered, "we risk being left with only crumbs when we are finally forced to negotiate with the enemy." But no-one appeared to be interested – Savory was pilloried as a traitor and a sell-out.

However, as I listened to Savory's words, heard him argue that continuing the war was simply hardening the enemy's resolve, a veil lifted from my eyes. With new-found clarity, I suddenly understood what it must be like to be black and to endure daily insults and discrimination. I realised that if I walked in an African's shoes, my indignation would also quickly turn to anger, and I, too, would soon be casting around for a way to retaliate. It dawned on me that if Savory was right, and Africans turned against us en masse, my own future and that of all white

Rhodesians, was at grave risk. In a youthful rush of panic, I confronted my parents:

"Mum, Dad, please will you vote for Savory in the election. Everything he says makes perfect sense. The Rhodesian Front will destroy this country if they continue with this war. We can't afford to go down this route. We have to change course, if it's not too late already!"

My mother did not answer immediately, but instead glanced at my father, who said nothing. For a moment, I interpreted my parents' silence to mean they were actually considering my request. Then my mother took a deep breath.

"We know you feel strongly about this, dear," she addressed me gently, "but we've had faith in Ian Smith this far, and we still think he will sort things out for the best. We will be voting for Smith."

I was distraught. Too young to vote, powerless to influence even my parents, let alone the wider political landscape, yet still fiercely proud of my country, I didn't know which way to turn. I felt trapped, like an impala in a spotlight, unable to avoid the inevitable looming bullet.

Like my parents, the rest of the electorate also didn't share my concerns - on election day, Smith won all 50 electoral seats.

15 Didge

"Security Forces regret to announce the death in action of Corporal...."

The terse announcement at the beginning of the evening newscast never failed to stop conversation. It was an increasingly frequent reminder that the true cost of our escalating conflict was increasingly being paid in destroyed lives.

And these were young lives.

"Did you hear about Didge?" someone asked. Didge was our previous Head Boy and had been captain of the First Team Rugby. Like many others, he'd been called up for National Service once he'd completed his education.

"No. What happened?"

"Didge is in hospital. Not good. Turned over a dead terrorist and a concealed grenade went off in his face, poor bugger."

I was shocked. It was the first time that someone close to me had become a victim of the war. A war that had previously seemed distant and abstract and academic, suddenly was brought alarmingly close and real and touchable. An image of Didge's smashed body now mocked me endlessly from inside my head. With my school days drawing to a close and my own call-up imminent, I found myself worrying more and more whether fate hadn't got similar plans in store for me.

16 South Africa

It was with huge relief, therefore, that I received notification from the military agreeing to defer my National Service for four years to allow me to attend university in South Africa. For some obscure reason, the course I had chosen to study, town planning, was regarded by the Rhodesian government as essential to the war effort. Accordingly, from 1975 to 1978, I became one of a handful of Rhodesian school leavers who was allowed to enjoy my teenage years outside the country, away from the increasingly tense political situation at home.

My new home, Wits University in Johannesburg, offered an environment that I immediately relished. Gone were the strict protocols and infuriating petty rules of my school years, replaced by an astonishingly open and relaxed learning environment. Not only was there academic freedom at university, but the whole ethos of life there embraced tolerance of new ideas and unconventional thinking. To a boy coming from a society of Victorian censorship, conservative propaganda, and heavy-handed authority, it was a heady experience.

Naturally, once we realised that university was also as much about girls and alcohol as it was about passing end of year exams, my friends and I began to push the boundaries. During one holiday some of us decided to take a trip to the beaches of Sordwana Bay. We crammed four of us plus essential supplies (several crates of beers) into my old Vauxhall station wagon and headed for the Zululand coast.

After a long day's travel, we pulled into the small town of Eshowe, where we had arranged an overnight stop at Ian's family home. Ian's father made us welcome and after a hearty meal, we decided to find out what Eshowe had to offer in the way of night life. Borrowing his dad's car, Ian drove us towards town. Suddenly a figure in a reflective vest jumped out into the beam of our headlights, waving us down.

"A bloody speed trap," muttered Ian. He pulled the car over, got out, and walked over to where the cop was standing next to his radar. After a few moments, Ian returned. He leaned in the window. "He's going to fine me for doing 62 *kays* in a 60 zone," he said disgustedly,

"What!? That's ridiculous. What's wrong with the guy?"

"They call this fellow Mickey Mouse," snorted Ian, jerking his thumb in the direction of the policeman. "He's the local traffic cop here, and he thinks he's God. He's always completely unreasonable. One little thing, and he's all over you. "

"Well, this is just plain stupid," said Trent from the back seat. "You can't give someone a ticket for doing just two *kays* over the limit." He jumped out the car and he and Ian went back to where the policeman was writing out the ticket. Through the window we watched as Trent gesticulated wildly at the policeman. A few moments later, he too returned to the car.

"What a prick!" Trent spat.

"What happened?"

"He told me to get back in the car, or he would put all of us in the cells for the weekend! The guy's a complete jerk."

Ian came back to the car carrying a ticket. "50 rand," he muttered darkly. "You know, he does this all the time.

He's the only traffic cop in this piss place, and he thinks
he's God. People here hate him."

We carried on to the pub, but the evening was
already spoiled. A dark mood settled on all of us. We played
pool and drank beers until closing time.

"So, do you know where this traffic cop lives?"
queried Grant.

"Sure," Ian replied. "This place is just a village."

"Let's go and have a look then."

We cruised through the empty, darkened streets.
"There," said Ian after a while, pointing to a house set well
back from the road.

"Well, what do you know, there's his little piss cop
car as well." Sure enough, a blue police vehicle was parked
in a carport at the side of the house.

"Bugger it. I'm gonna teach that turd a lesson," said
Trent, opening his door.

Grant giggled, "Me too, hang on." Before I could
suggest we discuss it further, Grant and Trent had hopped
out the car, and were bobbing across the darkened lawn.

"Shit, Ian," I muttered, "those idiots mean it. You'd
better keep the engine running. We might have to get out of
here in a hurry."

We watched the two drunken students weave across
the grass. They were headed towards the police car.

"Not the car, please," I whispered to myself.

At the last minute the two shadowy figures seemed
to hesitate, confer, then changed direction, moving to the
front of the house. There was a pause – at this distance I
couldn't see properly – then came the distant sound of
tinkling glass.

"Shit, what have they done?"

As we watched, the two figures came rushing back across the lawn. They wrenched open the rear door and tumbled into the back seat on top of each other.

"Go! Go!" shouted Trent. Ian didn't need any encouragement. He floored the accelerator, and headed up the street. I addressed the two giggling heaps lying in the backseat.

"What the fuck did you do?"

"We chucked bricks right through his lounge window," Trent laughed delightedly. "Gee, it made a noise. That'll teach the prick."

"Hee, hee!" sniggered Grant's floundering body from somewhere underneath Trent.

"You *ous* are *penga*," I shouted. "Mad! The guy gives us a ticket tonight, then you do this! It won't take much for him to put two and two together."

"You know," said Ian with remarkable restraint, "I think we'd better leave town first thing in the morning."

17 Differing Opinions

In spite of all our carousing in South Africa, the politics of Rhodesia still managed to impinge on our carefree student existence. The steadily escalating war at home raised tensions among Rhodesian students whenever the topic was broached. One day, at a faculty cheese and wine function, I was spouting off some liberal opinion on the war, when I noticed Tony, another Rhodesian, standing on the fringe of the conversation. It looked like Tony was getting more and more riled at what I was saying. *Bugger him*, I thought. I wasn't about to tone down my views just to please his conservative sensitivities – I'd had enough of censorship back home, and was enjoying the freedom of expression permitted at university.

After a while, we left the party. I found myself following Tony down some steps. Perhaps I made another barbed remark. Or perhaps Tony's simmering anger just exploded. Whichever, I suddenly found Tony grabbing me by the front of my collar, and screaming, "You just shut up, hey! You don't know what the fuck you're talking about." His grip on my collar was like a vice. His voice trembled with rage. "You just have no idea! No fucking idea at all." The fingers at my throat were like steel springs. I knew, then, that he was about to deck me.

My reaction was partly instinct, partly calculated. I lifted up my arm, then brought it down on Tony's head. In my hand, the two-litre wine bottle I was carrying smashed into a spray of glass fragments and wine.

Tony dropped like a book, and lay motionless on the steps. There was a stunned silence from the other students.

I nudged the inert form at my feet. Nothing. Had I killed him? "Tony, Tony, wake up!" I shook his shoulder.

"Whaaat……what happened?" Thank God he was coming round. But he was out of it.

"It's okay, Tony, it's okay." He wasn't. There was blood gushing out of a deep cut on his head.

"What… happened?"

"Tony, someone hit you. You're hurt. We've got to get you to hospital."

Suddenly aware of all the blood on him, Tony was distracted long enough for us to staunch the bleeding and get him to my car. But as we drove to hospital, he started questioning me again: "What happened? Who hit me?"

"Just a friend, Tony. I'll tell you all about it tomorrow. Let's just get you stitched up first."

"Tell me."

"It was just one of your friends. He was pissed. You don't want to know, not tonight. We're all pissed, it'll just make things worse. I'll tell you tomorrow, I promise." I wasn't sure if I was more concerned about Tony's amnesia, or more relieved that he couldn't remember my role as his assailant. But I certainly didn't want to start the argument all over again. Especially now that I had run out of wine bottles!

Another incident occurred that unsettled me much more. I had joined a student newspaper, and had been asked to write an article on a recent "pre-emptive" strike that Rhodesian forces had made on Nyadzonya guerrilla camp in Mozambique. Over a thousand Africans were reported dead in the attack, including large numbers of women and children. Of course, there was no way for me to visit the area or interview anyone who had been involved, so I had to rely on other sources to compile my article. There were clearly two versions of the event: the Rhodesian government press release claimed the camp was a terrorist training base, and that everyone killed in the assault had been intimately involved in terrorist activities or training. Other versions of the incident, particularly in the overseas media, were claiming that the camp was populated almost entirely by refugees. The Rhodesians were accused of slaughtering hundreds of unarmed civilians.

Unable to determine the truth of either claim, I decided I should write a balanced article, citing both perspectives. My article was supported with graphic photographs of the bodies of the dead which I managed to obtain courtesy of a local newspaper.

The day my article appeared in the student paper, I was walking up the front steps towards the residence dining room when I saw someone pointing at me. A moment later, a tall, scowling individual stood before me. He wore tight shorts, and his cropped hair was thinning, too soon for his age. He sure looked like trouble.

"Graham Atkins?"

"Yes," I replied warily.

"You wrote that article about the terrorist camp in Mozambique."

"Uh-huh."

"My name's Pat. I'm here to tell you that what you wrote is a complete load of crap." No beating around the bush here, then.

"I'm sorry you feel that way," I said, "everyone's entitled to their opinion."

"It's not my opinion," he spluttered. "What you wrote is completely wrong." The muscles in his jaw twitched.

"Completely?"

"You said it was a refugee camp. That's bullshit. It was a terrorist base"

I started to explain. "I didn't ..."

He cut me off. "How can you say something like that? You're a Rhodesian. You're supposed to be patriotic!"

"I am," I replied, trying to keep my tone as even as possible, "that doesn't mean that I have to accept everything the government says as gospel."

"But you weren't even there!" he exploded. "I've fought in the war. I know what these *gondies* are like, man! Have you been in the army? No! So you know fuck all."

I started to say something, but he cut me off again.

"Listen, man," he said, his voice dropping, as if letting me in on something too dreadful to say out loud, "these *gooks* torture people, and burn them alive. They rape young girls just for fun. They cut off people's ears and lips. I tell you, they're just fucking animals. They train women and kids as terrorists, and send them out to murder our farmers. *That's* why we hunt them down and kill them, wherever they are."

I could taste the venom in his every word. Interested onlookers were jostling around to see if our debate would erupt into a fight. I tried to stay calm. How could I understand the emotional scars that battle had inflicted on this man? Battles that I couldn't even start to imagine.

"I'm not saying you're wrong," I argued. "All I said in my article is that there are two sides to this story. I reported your side, and I reported the guerrillas' side. What's wrong with that?"

"Don't you fuckin' ever again call those bastards *guerrillas*," he spat. "Those *munts* in the camps are not guerrillas. They are not refugees. They're terrorists, plain and simple."

"Okay," I said. "Thanks for your views. We seem to have different opinions. I guess we'll just have to leave it at that." For a moment it looked as if he was about to go and the crowd thinned in disappointment. Then he spun round again.

"You don't get it, do you? They hate you as much as they hate me. They hate all of us whites, and all they want is to get rid of you and your family and destroy everything you own. You can moralise as much as you want about seeing both sides. But at the end of the day, to them, your family is white, and while you sit here in South Africa criticising, back home it's only our soldiers that are keeping your family safe."

Top: Martin, me, Mum and Dad

Above: Me, aged 1

Centre: my family at Scottburgh beach

Right: Martin (left), me (centre) and cousins Anne, Louise and Peter John

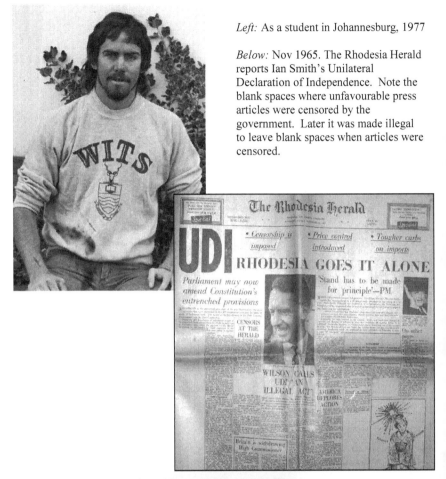

Left: As a student in Johannesburg, 1977

Below: Nov 1965. The Rhodesia Herald reports Ian Smith's Unilateral Declaration of Independence. Note the blank spaces where unfavourable press articles were censored by the government. Later it was made illegal to leave blank spaces when articles were censored.

Left: As students on tour in the Eastern Transvaal, 1978. Bruce Kerswill, Martin Evans, Tom Pressinger, and me

18 The Beginning of the End

Whatever our differing views on campus, back home across the border, things for the Rhodesians were going from bad to worse. In 1975 the Portuguese abandoned their colony of Mozambique, leaving Rhodesia's entire eastern flank completely exposed to rebel activity. It didn't take the insurgents long to exploit this vacuum – they established several training camps just inside the Mozambique border, and began to launch cross-border sorties into the mountainous eastern districts. Umtali was mortared, the first time a Rhodesian city had come under attack (the attacks were more symbolic than militarily significant - after one attack, residents awoke to find that some wag had pulled out some plants on the city's flower clock and changed the wording from "Welcome to Umtali", to "We come to Umtali").

While Rhodesians still tried to maintain an air of normality, there was no doubt that the pressure was starting to mount. The much vaunted minefield along the Mozambique border was proving an ineffective defence, and on the main roads in the east and south, civilian vehicles now had to travel in armed convoys. National service for school leavers was extended from one year to eighteen months, and then to two years. A significant blow to morale came when the South African government announced it would no longer support Rhodesia with troops, and withdrew the police details that had been assisting with border patrols. And financially, the direct costs of defending the country were now consuming twenty percent of the country's budget, while at the same time businesses were grinding to a standstill due to a lack of manpower, materials and investment.

South Africa and the Front-line states – Zambia, Botswana, Mozambique – now realised that an ongoing civil war in Rhodesia was detrimental to their own interests. They agreed to bring pressure to bear on the protagonists, and in 1976, Smith and the nationalists were forced to the negotiating table.

This time South Africa meant business. They told Smith that unless he signed a deal with black leaders, South Africa would withdraw all support for Rhodesia and would cut off the country's vital oil and trade links. Smith felt totally betrayed.

Mugabe and Nkomo, however, decided against any peaceful compromise and pulled out of the negotiations in favour of continuing the war. For once, Smith had an opportunity to seize the moral high ground; after more months of tortuous negotiations, he brokered a settlement with a group of moderate black leaders. In a national broadcast, Smith announced that he had secured a deal that would restore the country to international favour, end sanctions, and guarantee the future of whites in the country. What exactly was the ground-breaking deal? "We have agreed," Smith revealed, "to the election of a black government based on universal suffrage."

The white electorate that had supported Smith for so long was stunned. This man, who had only a few months earlier told them that he did "not believe in majority rule …not in a thousand years", now appeared to have done a complete U-turn – it seemed to many to be a total surrender.

Smith guided the country to its first non-racial elections and in 1979 Bishop Abel Muzorewa was elected the country's first black Prime Minister. But hopes that this

would end the country's international pariah status were
soon dashed. Despite this being the first democratic change
of government on the African continent for 25 years, the
UN and the rest of the world refused to recognise a
government that did not include the recalcitrant Nkomo and
Mugabe.

For white Rhodesians, it seemed that events had
played out in the worst scenario imaginable – they had
abdicated political power to the black majority, yet there
was no peace dividend as a reward. Instead, Prime Minister
Muzorewa was now pleading with whites and the military
not to abandon their country at this critical stage. The only
problem was, most Rhodesians, black or white, now no
longer knew who or what they were supposed to be fighting
for.

19 Call-up

"Your call-up papers have arrived." My dad's voice crackled down the international telephone link to the call-box at my university residence.

It was the news I had been expecting all year, but which I had hoped, somehow, fate would defer.

20 Into Uniform

When I received news of my call-up, my first impulse was to "take the gap" into self-imposed exile and to wait out the final play of the Rhodesian drama from afar. In fact, I did take a flight to London - but it didn't take long for the British winter to force me to rethink my options. I was soon on the phone to my parents announcing stridently that it was preferable to be shot at by terrorists in sunny Rhodesia than to spend one more day in the bitter cold, wet and general misery of mid-winter England.

Only my family knew of my decision to return home. It was February 1979, and the news from the war zone was grimmer than ever. As I alighted at Salisbury airport and my delighted family rushed to greet me, I was torn between feelings of relief at getting back to familiar territory, and trepidation about the uncertain future that I had opted for.

The next day, I headed for the Oasis Motel, a popular weekend hangout for young people. I knew I would find my friends drinking there. I walked through the wrought-iron gates, past flowering scented frangipanis and into the hubbub of the beer-garden. In the sunshine and surrounded by familiar accents, I felt at home again. I recognised several friends and waved cheerily.

"Graham! You've come back!" My friends couldn't believe their eyes. They'd written me off as just another draft dodger. Now they slapped me on the back, shook my hand, and badgered me for explanations.

I played up my response. "I'd rather face the *gooks* than drink any more of that warm UK beer," I joked.

"You missed your call-up. Aren't you in deep *kak*?"

"Don't worry about the army, I can handle them," I smirked, oozing bravado. What I didn't reveal was that I already knew the army had taken the pragmatic view - desperate for every pair of hands it could muster, my delay in reporting for duty had already been forgiven.

I knew coming back was a risk, that the war was entering a critical stage, and that casualties were rising. But I had the overwhelming feeling that I was at last playing a role in history, not running away from it any more. That feeling, and the effusive welcome of my loyal friends, seemed to wash away any trepidation.

A few days later, sporting a short back-and-sides haircut, I arrived at Llewellin Barracks, Bulawayo, along with hundreds of other new recruits, for the start of my one year call-up. I was greeted by a scene out of a boot camp movie: gawky recruits sporting shorn heads were being herded into lines. There was shouting and swearing, and a mixture of testosterone and nerves filled the air. The strong tang of dust, diesel fumes, and camp latrines carried on the breeze.

At least half the recruits were black. With the recent scrapping of racial laws, the call-up had been extended to include young blacks with O-Level qualifications. I wondered how they must feel, being conscripted into a war against their own people? Perhaps they had good reason to look even more nervous than the white recruits.

We were sorted into groups, issued with ill-fitting camouflage uniforms, given even shorter haircuts, and put through a perfunctory medical examination. Thereafter, it was a daily routine of running, climbing, drill and standing at attention for hours in the hot sun. The spotty-faced corporals in charge of us looked younger than me, barely out of school. They flung insults and abuse, taking sadistic pleasure in our discomfort. At night, lying on my bunk, I could hear the sound of stifled sobs drifting through the barracks. There was a rumour of an attempted suicide.

Towards the end of the first week, we were made to negotiate a tangle of obstacle courses and team challenges, and sit IQ tests. After the tests, a clean-cut officer wearing captain's pips addressed a small group of us. "I'm looking for volunteers for officers' training," he announced.

In my mind I replayed advice I had picked up from somewhere - *Don't volunteer for anything* - and kept silent. My hope was to somehow wangle my way into the medics, or radio operations, services which, it seemed to me, would be well away from dangerous "sharp end" war duties.

The officer in charge spoke again, "I still need one more volunteer for officer training. Come on, you are all great candidates in this room." He looked straight at me as he said it. I sat still. The officer walked over to me, and called me aside. His manner was friendly yet sincere. "Listen, son, you're a bright one, and you're older than most of these other kids. We need someone like you to lead these guys. Won't you please reconsider?"

"It's not something I had planned on doing."

"Look at it this way," he continued," you can either spend your time in the army with people younger and less competent than you telling you what to do, one of these kids maybe," - he waved his arm around the room - "or you can be the one who gives the orders. Which would you prefer?"

I pondered a moment. Would it change my life? Would there be regrets? Who could tell. I stood up. "OK, what the hell, I'll go."

I joined a group of other recruits who had also been selected for officer training, and we drove the two hour trip to the School of Infantry. Nestling at the foot of the Gwelo *kopje* and guarded by a simple red-and-white painted boom gate, the camp had an unprepossessing appearance. We debussed and lined up in front of a tall, gangly man with a droopy black moustache.

"Captain du Plooy is my name, and this," he announced, indicating a short, crew-cut soldier standing ram-rod stiff at attention, "is your course instructor, Sergeant van Vuuren. Listen well to what he tells you – it *will* save your life."

The small sergeant stepped crisply to the front of our squad. Taut muscles bulged under his shirt.

"164 Alpha – Atten-shun!" We shuffled to attention, the recruit next to me wobbling precariously as he did so.

"WHAT…WAS…THAT?!" the sergeant roared into the face of the rookie. The boy flinched under the whip of the Afrikaans accent.

"By the time you have finished working with me," the sergeant lifted his eyes to take us all in, "you will be the best drill squad ever to pass out of this school. Do you understand?"

"Yes, Sergeant," we all responded.

"I can't hear you!"

"YES, Sergeant!"

"I still can't hear you!"

"YES, SERGEANT!!"

21 Training

Sergeant van Vuuren was true to his word. Drill, we discovered, was his passion. Even though the reality of war had significantly reduced the army's traditional emphasis on spit and polish, there was no way that our sergeant was going to compromise on parade ground skills. We soon found ourselves marching up and down the parade ground hour after hour. When other squads had been allowed back into their barracks, we were kept on the drill ground to rehearse our movements over and over: left-turns, about-turns, halt, port arms, quick march, the lot.

At first, we were your typical bumbling rookies - some of us wheeled left while others wheeled right. Some of us marched on, while others halted. Bit by bit, however, we started to find our rhythm - our movements became smarter, and our steps more precise.

Unfortunately for Sergeant van Vuuren, he had been burdened with one rookie who was completely unable to master even the simplest drill. Private Rosenhall was a sunburnt, stocky individual whose family were influential farmers from the Plumtree area. As our drill training progressed it became more and more obvious to our sergeant that Rosenhall was the weak link in his plan to produce a quality drill squad. When the sergeant commanded our squad to turn to the left, Rosenhall would go right. When he commanded us to halt, Rosenhall would stop on the wrong foot. The lad couldn't even coordinate a simple marching action. Instead of marching with his arms moving counter to his legs, Rosenhall's left arm would sail out at the same time as his left leg; then his right arm and right leg would move together. It was like watching a toy robot trying to walk after it had been wrongly assembled.

At first, the sergeant screamed and shouted at Rosenhall, but this just seemed to make the recruit more nervous, and he made even more mistakes. Then the sergeant resorted to punishing our whole squad whenever Rosenhall made a mistake, in the hopes that peer pressure could cure him. Every time Rosenhall turned the wrong way, our whole squad would be sent running to the top of the *kopje*, while Rosenhall stood at attention on the parade ground. When he failed to halt on cue, we all had to do fifty push-ups, while Rosenhall was made to watch. Exhausted, it wasn't long before we were threatening the apologetic recruit with the worst imaginable beatings if he made another mistake. But it had no effect – Rosenhall was simply hard-wired to march out of step.

Sergeant van Vuuren, apoplectic with rage, finally gave up, and stormed off to the CO's office. There was an uneasy silence as we waited in the gathering gloom of the parade ground. Eventually we were dismissed, and returned to our barracks.

The next day, there was no sign of Rosenhall. Someone said he had been RTU'd to Llewellin. It was probably true, but I wasn't sure that our sergeant hadn't at least considered a more spectacular end for the unfortunate boy.

While the army, by 1979, had fully embraced non-racialism, in civilian life, society was taking longer to adjust. This was brought home one Saturday when we received a rare day pass to go into town. A small group of us had set off in search of entertainment. We started with a syrup-covered waffle at a popular café, the Dutch Oven. From one of the girls there we learnt of a wedding reception in progress at the local church hall. The rumour of free booze was all the encouragement we needed. As we were already wearing ties and jackets, we were confident we would be able to sneak in to the reception unobserved, so we set off in the direction of the party.

The reception was in full swing when we arrived. Then we remembered we had a problem – Moses, our good-humoured comrade-in-arms, was black. Trying to get Moses in to the wedding unobserved would be like…well, like trying to smuggle a black man into a white wedding.

When he realised this dilemma, Moses' face fell. "You guys go in without me," he sighed.

"Hang on a moment," I said, and disappeared in the direction of the bar. A few seconds later, I returned, brandishing a silver tray and a white napkin. "Your ticket in," I said to Moses.

"What?"

"It's simple. Put on your best impersonation of a waiter, and you'll blend in perfectly."

The ruse worked. Disguised as a waiter, Moses became instantly invisible. He slipped in the back door undetected and before long he was circulating effortlessly through the crowd of white revellers, wielding his silver tray with aplomb, swapping banter with the groom and guests, and enjoying the music.

We decided we couldn't let him get away with it that easily. "Hey, waiter, six beers, please. *Checha!* Quick!"

22 The Thing about Girls

One of the hardest things for me to adapt to in the army was the almost complete absence of women. Frustrated by the male oriented confines of camp, I desperately sought out even the smallest social contact with the opposite sex. One day, I managed to strike up a conversation with the Commanding Officer's teenage daughter as she played tennis on the camp tennis court. After some light banter, the leggy blonde invited me and a buddy into her parents' house for coffee. Unfortunately, before we even got beyond the pleasantries, the girl's mother spotted us and we were quickly booted out. Presumably as punishment for my audacity, I soon found myself posted to an unscheduled week of night-time guard duty. As the cold winter air blew down my neck, and I stamped my feet to keep warm, I found myself with plenty of time to ponder the vexing issue of girls…

…The first girl that I remember being totally smitten with was Deborah Harley. At the time we were both twelve years old. Deborah, tall, dark-haired, and statuesque, was a veritable Cleopatra to my eyes. Although we were in the same class at school, we might as well have been on different planets for all the attention she gave me. The only thing that Deborah and I ever had in common was that we were once swept out to sea together. It happened during a holiday at the seaside. On the day in question, the waves were particularly rough, with a vicious undertow, but because of the hot weather there were scores of people swimming in the sea. I recognised Deborah instantly when I spotted her swimming near to me. Yellow droplets of sun sparkled like jewels in her hair, and her long golden arms made me quiver all over.

Unfortunately, before I had time to work out how I was going to approach her, I felt the undercurrent catch me. Before I knew it, I was being swept out beyond the rocky headland. I panicked, looking around for help. Suddenly, there was Deborah, just metres from me. We had both been swept in the same direction, while all the other bathers had been swept the opposite way. The life-savers had their hands full rescuing the larger group, so it seemed to me that Deborah and I would have to save ourselves. I had a fleeting vision of myself heroically performing the role of rescuing this damsel in distress. Unfortunately, my dream foundered as quickly as I nearly did. I'm not the world's best swimmer. Swallowing lungfuls of salt water, it was all I could do to stay afloat. My last thought: *Who will save Deborah?*

After battling the current for ages, I finally hauled myself exhausted onto the sand. I lay there, gasping for breath. To my surprise, Deborah was already back at the beach, watching the life-savers rescue the other swimmers. God, what a magnificent girl, I thought to myself. Then I realised this was my chance. Panicked, I wondered what to say.

"Well, that was hard work," I finally panted out, smiling up at her like a drowned dog. Deborah turned, noticing me at her feet for the first time. I don't think she had a clue who I was.

"Yah," she replied, her eyes returning to the life-savers, "Jeez, look at that. People shouldn't be allowed out there if they can't swim." Then she strode off down the beach to see if she could help. It was the closest I ever got to having a conversation with her.

When I was thirteen, I moved to the cloistered walls of Churchill Boys High School. Our sister school, Roosevelt Girls High, was just down the road, but it might as well have been on another planet for all the contact we were allowed with its inmates. At a time when I was entering puberty and ready to learn some social skills, all contact with girls was suddenly severed – I was left to observe them from a distance, as if they were some exotic and distant species.

The one chance for Churchill boys to meet some of our Roosevelt peers was at the school dance. However, with almost no experience of social interaction with the fairer sex, and consumed with trepidation, self-doubt and feelings of inadequacy, I spent most of the school dance with my equally shy class-mates lurking on the outskirts of the action. Eventually, I plucked up the nerve to ask a girl to dance. I don't remember her name, but I do remember that she had soft dark hair and a gentle smile. Most vividly, though, I remember our slow dance together. As the music slowed and the lights dimmed, we moved closer. I put my arms around her alien form and held her tight, conscious of the softness of her skin and the delicious smell of her hair. We shuffled around the floor, and it was pure bliss. I prayed for the music to never stop. Unfortunately, the soft lighting, the girl's pheromones, and our close body contact, all proved to be a heady combination and I was suddenly aware of something awakening in my trousers. The more I tried to ignore it, the more persistent it became. Soon there was no hiding things any more. The poor girl stopped our slow shuffle abruptly, gave me a look like death, and hurried off for the safety of her giggling girlfriends. Hugely embarrassed, I ducked out a side door and fled home.

Later, when I went to university, I became more used to having girls around. I overcame my earlier debilitating shyness, learnt how to hold a conversation with a girl and even managed some passable attempts at flirting. The spice and tension of being close to the opposite sex was exciting. However, I found myself continually frustrated as my relationships never seemed to get beyond the platonic stage. Inside, I yearned to get close to a girl, to experience love and passion.

Occasionally, I met someone that I prayed would turn out to be my Miss Right: one potential candidate, I felt, was Linda Cook. Linda was sophisticated, with Hollywood starlet looks. When I was first introduced, my heart did an immediate flip, and I spent the next few months manufacturing chance meetings and trailing after Linda like a puppy. She was always kind and friendly towards me, but it was all to no avail - I was politely yet resolutely kept at arms length.

Then there was Kirstene Ralph. Sultry, with curves in all the right places, Kirstene loved my jokes and had a wonderfully vivacious outlook on life. It all looked very promising at first – then I took my eye off her for just a moment and she slipped through my fingers.

The next promising candidate was Helen Dewhurst. With a voice of pure silk and a laugh that bubbled up from deep inside, Helen stole my heart with her first words…

…I snapped out of my day-dreams and back to the present. Frost had settled on the bonnets of the army trucks I was supposed to be guarding and the freezing June night air had chilled me through to the bone. I muttered morosely. Pondering my love-life, or rather the lack of it, had left me grumpy and filled with self-pity. Indeed, on the eve of my going off to war, it looked like my virginity was going to remain depressingly intact.

The next day, the army gave us a weekend pass. Overjoyed at the chance to taste civvy-street night life again, I was soon back in Salisbury. However, the long stretch of guard duty the previous night had left me dog-tired and irritable. I contemplated not going out with my friends, and just getting a good night's sleep. Then the phone rang. I answered curtly, far from my sociable best.

"Yes?"

"Hello big *boet.*" My brother's cheerful voice floated over the static. What with university and the war, Martin and I hadn't seen much of each other recently. "I heard you were in town, *boetie.* Listen, Ilse and I are going out to dinner at Mono's, and we'd like you to come along." In spite of my tiredness, I wanted to see my brother again, so I grumpily accepted the invitation.

"See you at seven, then," said Martin. Then he added casually, "Oh, by the way, we've invited a special guest to join us."

"Who?"

Martin feigned intrigue. "Oh, you'll find out soon enough." Then he added conspiratorially, "You've met her before."

"What? You mean a girl?"

There was a click as the phone hung up.

"Bastard," I said into the hiss of the dead line.

I arrived promptly at seven. The Monomatapa hotel, its sweeping bulk overlooking the city's central gardens, had survived the war years by focusing on its food and drink trade. The restaurants and pubs were jam-packed with locals enjoying themselves, keen to banish for a few hours all thoughts of the war.

"Good evening sir." The *maitre d'*, impeccable in black suit and bow tie, greeted me.

"Table for Atkins."

"Ah, yes, sir. Your brother is expecting you. Please follow me."

I was ushered towards the far side of the room. I caught sight of Martin and his girl-friend Ilse seated at a table in the corner, and waved to them. A third person was sitting with them, a girl with dark shoulder length hair. Her bare shoulders were turned away from me, and in the dim lighting, I couldn't make out her face.

"There he is!" said my brother warmly, rising to greet me.

"Hi, *boet*. Hi Ils." I greeted Ilse with a kiss on the check and shook my brother's hand. Then Martin turned to introduce my date. From behind a cascade of chestnut hair, the mystery girl looked up at me. Candlelight caught her high cheek-bones, and flickered down a provocative cleavage.

"Hello, Graham," she said, a smile flickering behind the low voice. "You remember me, don't you?"

23 An Unexpected Encounter

I certainly did remember her.

It had been six months earlier. My university friends Tom, Mart, and I had been on a booze-fuelled holiday, and had stopped over in Salisbury. At the time, Ilse was a drill-sergeant in the women's army service. When she heard I was in town, she invited my friends and I to a recruits' passing-out party at Army HQ. Presented with a chance to enter the heart of the famous Rhodesian military machine, it was too good an opportunity for us "*commie*" students to miss - we accepted the invitation immediately. Besides, we had also heard that the army charged just thirty cents for a beer!

We arrived at army HQ ready to rock and roll. The party was already off to a lively start, the female recruits dancing with each other and downing beers as fast as they could. Their "live-for-today" attitude perfectly complemented our own buoyant holiday mood, and soon the party was in full swing. That many of the army girls appeared to be "gay" did nothing to dampen our spirits – we joined in the festivities with abandon, and soon everyone was having a wild time.

After a while I noticed a startlingly attractive girl across the room.

"Who's that?" I asked.

"Ah! Let me introduce you." Ilse crossed the floor, and brought the girl back with her. "This is my senior officer. But you guys can call her Debby, seeing's how you're not in the army. I warn you, however, Debby and I make a mean drinking team, so don't even *think* of taking us on."

We all introduced ourselves. I was instantly attracted to this newcomer – she had smouldering good looks, quick wit, and total confidence - and I was doubly impressed with the fact that she also held the rank of Captain. My 'varsity buddies were also impressed. Here was a level of female talent they had not previously associated with the army. I noticed we all immediately stepped up our macho displays a notch, retold our wittiest jokes, and attempted to flirt outrageously with this new girl. She took it all in her stride, keeping a cool control, but laughing gaily at our tales, matching our flirtatious comments, and pacing us drink for drink. I tried to catch her eye as often as possible.

The hours passed quickly, and in spite of consuming one too many beers, I decided to make a hopeful pitch. I broke in to the conversation: "Excuse me, Debby, how about you and me going out for dinner sometime?"

She paused in mid joke, turned and regarded me intently. The look she gave me was unmistakable - she clearly thought I was a lunatic.

"What? What's wrong?" I protested, looking to my friends for guidance. "Hell's bells, it's just a dinner invitation, I didn't ask you to marry me!"

"No," she replied, breaking into laughter, "but somebody else already did." She lifted a hand and waved it under my nose. On her perfectly tanned finger, a wedding ring gleamed gold in the yellow light.

"Oh," was all I could say.

Tom and Mart, bless them, thought it was the funniest joke of our trip.

"Hello, Debby. It's great to see you again," I said, leaning past my brother and shaking her hand. I was still in shock. What, I asked myself as I looked her up and down, was this goddess doing here as my dinner partner?

We sat down and ordered drinks. As we waited for the waiter to return, I blurted out, "I thought you were married?"

Debby glanced at me. "I was," she replied casually, "but I'm in the middle of a divorce."

"Great," I said. "Er, I mean, let's have a bottle of wine. Just to wish you good luck and all."

So dinner and my blind date had started out on a high note, and my hopes for a successful evening were high. However, I hadn't factored in the lack of sleep and physical punishment my body had taken during training over the past couple of weeks. As the smoky atmosphere and the wine took effect, I began to wilt. Within an hour, my eyelids were like lead, and I could feel my brain shutting down. *Not tonight*, I prayed, but I knew it was hopeless. I was simply too exhausted. Bit by bit I slumped lower in my seat, finally not even finding the energy to keep up with the dinner conversation.

Debby glanced at me with concern. "Are you okay?"

I realised what a poor impression I must be making on my date. "I'm fine, just a bit tired," I replied moodily.

Thirty minutes later, scarcely able to keep my eyes open, I bowed to the inevitable, made my apologies and went home for some desperately needed sleep.

After my poor showing the previous night, I was convinced that Debby wouldn't be interested in seeing me again. Nevertheless, on the off-chance, I gave her a call.

"I'd love to come out with you," she replied to my enquiry.

"Really? I'll pick you up at eight, then."

I could hardly wait for evening to come. When I pulled up outside her house, she opened the door and walked towards me. She looked stunning. As she climbed into the car, I couldn't help glancing at her long tanned legs

"I thought we would go to a party I've heard of."

"Fine. Let's go."

As we drove, I tried to make polite talk. But something was still bugging me. I tried to phrase the question casually. "I thought I blew it the other night. I'm surprised you agreed to come out with me again?"

"Are you kidding?" she replied.

"Well, I thought perhaps…"

"Remember when we first met six months ago, at my recruits' party?"

I nodded. How could I forget?

"Well," she continued, "I thought then that you were just another guy. You know, a typical bloke, drinking too much, being loud and obnoxious, you know, normal male macho stuff." I winced. Personally I had been under the impression that it had gone rather well that night. At least up until the ring debacle.

"But," she continued, "last night at the restaurant… well, Graham, you were so… so different. Quiet. Pensive. You seemed to be thinking all the time. It's like you've changed into someone else. I'm intrigued. I want to know why. I want to know what's happened to you that's changed you so much."

I turned my head away so that she couldn't see my involuntary smile. "It was just the guard duty," I muttered under my breath.

"Pardon?"

"Er, nothing… Oh, look, we're here already."

I parked the car on the road verge, and we got out. From a nearby house came sounds of laughter and voices raised above disco music. We followed other party-goers up the driveway and climbed a flight of steps onto a wide veranda. Scores of people were mingling and chatting. A DJ was playing a track by Boston, and a few couples were dancing. I recognized some old school acquaintances, waved, and headed towards the bar.

"Debby, how are you!" A guy in an open necked shirt launched himself at her, beaming, planting a heavy kiss on her cheek. Others joined us. Soon we found ourselves at the centre of a small crowd of revellers, rubbing shoulders and swaying to the music. Jokes and laughter ebbed and flowed easily, but I couldn't help noticing that most of the males were more interested in talking to my companion than to me. Wolves to a lamb. In a way, I supposed, it was a bit of a compliment, but I also knew I would have my work cut out keeping these damn wolves at bay.

After a while, Debby pulled me indoors, and we danced. I tried to play it cool, to project a casual air of indifference, but in the flashing lights, she looked sexier than ever. I found it hard to ignore the athletic legs tipped with high heeled shoes, the flashing smile, and the silky dark hair. I danced closer to her, and suddenly realised that beneath my practised look of studied calm, my stomach had tied itself in knots. I knew then that this was one girl that I didn't want to lose, didn't want to share with other men.

"There's too many people here," I said, drawing her aside by the waist. "Let's go back to the car. We can have our drinks in peace there."

"Sure," she replied. I felt my heart jump against my ribs.

We walked slowly back to the car, our arms brushing lightly. After the noise of the crowd, the quiet of the deserted street was like an oasis. Every step we took away from the party felt like a step closer to our own private sanctuary. Heavy winter dew was already settling on the grass. I opened the car door for her, and she slipped inside. Her taut brown calves flashed, and her black high-heels skewered the floor mat.

Once inside the car, we sipped our drinks, and talked - about the war, her job, my brother. The car windows gradually misted up, cocooning us, warm, away from everything else. She was funny and chatty, and I enjoyed just being there, alone, with her. I now knew this was just a prelude. I could sense the anticipation building between us. I glanced down. A glimpse of cleavage beckoned. I ran my hand along the curve of her thigh. She let it rest there, the warmth of her leg glowing through her skirt. I leaned towards her, smelt the woman-smell of her hair, then felt the silky touch of her fingers reaching for my neck. I looked deep into her eyes – there was a promise of everything in them.

"God, but you're beautiful," I murmured.

Her lips parted slightly and I could feel her breathing, shallow, urgent.

"Enough talking," she whispered. Then my lips were eagerly seeking hers, and we kissed, and I felt myself tumbling into forever.

24 Into the Whirlwind

I might have fallen hopelessly in love, but the war and the army weren't about to make any allowances for that. My officer training over, I was assigned to serve in the First Battalion of the Rhodesia Regiment. 1RR was an infantry unit that traced its proud origins back to the 1920's. The headquarters of 1RR was now the old Drill Hall, an austere colonial building whose red brick walls and colonnades had seen the comings and goings of military forces since early colonial days. I found my way to the armoury and was issued an FN rifle and ammunition. All around me activity continued at a frenzied pace: trucks pouring oily smoke stuttered and roared in every direction, and all about, soldiers bustled back and forth, sweating, harassed, urgent.

I was given my orders - take charge of a platoon of National Servicemen and proceed to base camp Pachanza somewhere in the north-east operational area. "There's a convoy leaving shortly," the Captain in charge said. "The men that you will command are waiting for you in those last two trucks." He pointed towards two armour-protected vehicles that crouched on the drill square like squat hyenas, their bullet-proof windows unblinking in the morning sun.

I walked towards the vehicles. It felt strange, walking by myself towards soldiers I didn't know – during our training in the School of Infantry, we had built 164 Alpha squad into a tight-knit unit whose team spirit was based on familiarity and mutual respect. Now we graduate officers from Intake 164 were scattered to the four corners of the armed forces, and I felt very much on my own again.

A cheerful greeting broke my reverie. "Good morning, Sir!"

I looked up into the first vehicle, squinting against the bright morning sun towards the strangely familiar voice.

"George! Is that you?"

"Sergeant Nolan to you, sir."

I couldn't believe my luck. George Nolan had been one of our coloured recruits in 164 Alpha. He had completed the training course with me, but had sadly only been awarded the rank of Sergeant. At the time, he must have been bitterly disappointed but, as he jumped down from the truck today, he showed no sign of that. He saluted me extravagantly.

"Cool it, George."

George pumped me with a traditional African triple hand-shake. "Welcome aboard, Graham."

"Boy, am I glad to see you," I replied. I meant it. I couldn't think of a better person to have as my right hand man going in to battle. "So tell me, what have we got here?"

"Shit, *my china*," George said, drawing me away by one arm, "what we've got here is a platoon of thirty fresh NS rookies, straight out of Llewellin training. Never been in the bush before."

"Well, that makes three of us," I joked awkwardly. I hadn't really expected anything else. I knew the army was scratching to find enough men to plug the holes in the war effort. They could no longer afford to get too fussy about who went where. "OK. Go on."

"Well, we've got two *honkies*, excluding you, you've got me as your Sergeant and token *goffel*, and then there are twenty seven Africans. Ushe is your Corporal. He seems okay. At least he's got a brain."

While I was digesting this information, and wondering how best to introduce myself to my troops, there was a sudden roar of engines, and the convoy ahead of us came to life. We coughed as oily diesel smoke enveloped us.

"Looks like we gotta go," said George. "You better take that vehicle, and I'll go in the rear one. We're apparently supposed to be at the back of the convoy, so's we can deploy if there's an ambush. My guess is, they just want us to eat everyone else's dust."

George turned to face the troops on the trucks. Above the noise of the revving vehicles he shouted, "Hey, you buggers, listen up! This is our new officer, Lieutenant Atkins. So now that's two of us that you gotta listen to, okay?"

I climbed into the back of the vehicle, and I could feel a dozen pairs of eyes giving me the once-over. George clambered aboard the other truck. An old joke flashed through my brain – *What did the sergeant say before the troops climbed in the trucks? "Right, troops, climb in the trucks."* But it didn't seem funny any more.

Our convoy eased out into the city traffic. As we did so, I heard George's voice raised above the revving engines. "Now buckle up, you cunts. And *don't* fucking cock your rifles until we're out of town!"

For a while our convoy travelled on a tarmac road, heading north. The city outskirts fell behind us, and small-holdings soon gave way to fertile farms stretching into the distance on either side. This was top-quality agricultural land, all of it owned by white commercial farmers. Maize and tobacco in tidy clipped rows waved their young leaves at us as we passed by, and embarrassed fat cattle buried their heads in the rich pastures. The pleasant scene, however, belied the fact that this area was now hotly contested terrain. The terrorists knew one thing - that if they could drive the white farmers off the land, the spirit of the Rhodesians would be broken.

After a couple of hours, we reached the small village of Mount Darwin, now a bustling military base where reckless army vehicles terrorised the sleepy inhabitants. We turned right, and headed north-east towards the Mozambique border. With a sudden thump, the tarmac road ended and the disciplined white farms immediately gave way to thin, scratched Tribal Trust Lands. Here the fields were small and stony and barren. Grass-fires smouldered along the roadside, lit by the security forces to clear potential ambush positions. The coffee-coloured smoke from the fires joined with the cloud of red dust spat out by our convoy. The red disc of the sun poked weakly through the grime. All beauty suddenly seemed to have been drained from the landscape. Reserved for the indigenous African population, the TTL's had always been the traditional front-line of the war. Now they looked more like ground zero. A mural of battered rural life flashed by. Desperate *pole-and-dagga* huts squatted like refugees along the road, or slumped, dazed, at the foot of scowling granite *kopjes*. Sad donkeys pulled carts filled with the corpses of the last remaining trees cut down for firewood. Behind the donkey carts trudged a seemingly endless procession of mute, thin women bearing pots of water on their heads. None of them acknowledged our passing.

I knew the civil war had begun over issues of equality, votes, and land. However, with the recent election of a black Prime Minister, like many whites I had hoped that the impetus for war would disappear. But gazing out at the bleak landscape, I realised that this war was far from over. Too much had been destroyed, too many lives ruined, too many hearts hardened. Everywhere, the burnt out shells of land-mined buses and wrecked donkey carts were grim testament to the bleeding, eroding lives of ordinary people now caught up in the hellish cross-fire between the power-mongers and the die-hards. As our convoy dusted past dead donkeys and sullen snotty-nosed kids, a great dread put its hands around my throat. We were well beyond any point of reason here. Now it was simply a fight to survive.

A *pookie* landmine detecting vehicle with broad fat tyres had joined the front of our convoy. Occasionally, when its driver detected something suspicious in the road surface, the *pookie* stopped and our convoy shuddered to a halt. Nervously we scanned the surrounding bush for an ambush. The driver of the *pookie,* looking more like an alien than a soldier in his flak-jacket and visored helmet, clambered awkwardly down from his mine-proof turret, and probed the red dirt with a small rod. We watched, holding our breath. Something was twitched from the road surface. The engineer peered at it, then satisfied, tossed it aside - a broken car-spring. The convoy crawled on.

By late afternoon, the large grey-purple massif of the Mavuradona mountains loomed to the north - dark, ominous, brooding. Beyond these mountains, I knew, spread the Zambezi valley, a shimmering hot-white swathe of *mopane* and scrub, infested with tsetse fly and thorn bush, cauldron of the modern guerrilla struggle, and nemesis of the white man.

Finally we broached the crest of a hill, and the skeleton of an abandoned school appeared ahead. There was no fence around the school, just the empty barren earth and low scrub extending towards the distant mountains. The buildings were roofless, the windows gone. A score of green army tents slumped nearby in the last of the day's heat, and a few beaten army trucks hunkered down in the dust. A "desert lily", a large metal funnel used as a communal urinal, protruded from the ground in an exposed position. The wind whipped up small dust-devils. I could make out slit trenches and sand-bagged mortar positions dotted about. Not a tree nor a blade of grass cheered the scene. So this was base camp. Our trucks bounced down the last eroded ruts and pulled up outside the shattered buildings. I clambered down from the truck, stretching my stiff limbs and heaving clean air into my polluted lungs. Home sweet home. Not.

The next morning I walked my men to a nearby patch of dusty ground that served as a rifle range. We spent the first hour testing our rifles and adjusting the sights.

"Now we'll practice skirmishing in pairs," I shouted. The first two soldiers came forward.

"What's your name, soldier?" I asked the taller one.

"Jacks, Sir."

"Okay, Jacks. The first man runs forward, and your buddy gives covering fire. Then swap. OK? You done this before?"

"I think so, sir."

I stood back to watch. I wanted to see if these rookies knew anything at all. Tomorrow we would be sent on patrol, and there would be no further chance to assess them until we had a real contact. Then it would be too late.

The two soldiers were nervous as hell. They lay on the ground, and fired a couple of jittery rounds at a distant bush.

"Skirmish!"

The first soldier got up into a crouch, ran forwards a few yards, then dived down.

"Now you, Jacks!"

Jacks stood up, his tall figure silhouetted against the skyline.

"It's supposed to be a skirmish, Jacks! Crouch and run!"

Suddenly there was a series of explosions next to me. I swung round to find George firing off rounds, aiming just above Jacks' head. It had the desired effect. Spurred on by the crack of bullets zipping past his ear, Jacks leapt into action. He dashed forward, zigzagging wildly across the open ground. I noticed puffs of white dust kicking up just inches in front of Jacks' feet.

"Better not aim so close, George."

"That's not me."

I looked again. Jacks was crouching and running hard, frantically trying to dodge the puffs of dust that tenaciously kept pace with his whirling feet.

"Shit, the idiot's got his finger on the trigger. He's dodging his own rounds!"

Stop! Stop!" I shouted. But by then there was no need. Jacks was already out of ammo.

25 The PV

I was pleasantly surprised by the warm welcome I and my platoon received at our new base camp. The major in charge went out of his way to personally show me around, making sure that I had a tent and a decent bed to sleep in. Now, as we inspected the slit trenches and mortar defences together, I warned the major that both I and my men were novices to live combat.

"I'm not sure how well my guys are going to shape up out there, sir."

The major raised an eyebrow, then replied, "The enemy overran the Valley a couple of years ago. The army basically pulled out to this side of the Mavuradona mountains, and the *Charlies* have pretty much had control over the valley ever since. Between the mountains" – he gestured to the purple hills behind us – "and the border minefield, it's effectively been part of Mozambique for years."

"I didn't realise that," I said.

"Well, the government has naturally never admitted it lost these border areas. But now they've decided it's important to show everyone that we still have effective control in every corner of the country. But do you know what that means?"

I shook my head. "No, sir."

"I've got one company of men, all of whom are civilians on call-up, and my instructions are to clear and secure an area the size of Northern Ireland!" He looked me in the eye. "So even if they sent me trained chimpanzees, I would be grateful."

Back in the operations tent, the major outlined my platoon's first mission. "A while back, the government came up with the idea of building Protected Villages. The idea of a PV is to fence the local peasants into a secure village, so that they can't give food to the *gooks* and so the *gooks* can't intimidate the locals at night. It's a policy that has had some tactical success, but..." He paused. We both knew there was controversy surrounding conditions in the PVs.

"Anyway," continued the major, "for the last couple of weeks, we've been moving all the locals we can find out of the valley, and into a new protected village behind this base camp. Internal Affairs runs the PV, but the District Commissioner has now requested our help to go back into the valley to collect the maize which is still there."

"You mean you want us to go and collect mealies?" I asked sceptically.

"That's exactly what you are going to do," replied the major soberly. "Every scrap you can find. If we don't, those *munts* in the PV are going to starve."

The Mavuradona mountains rose steeply to our left as we drove in convoy along the road that ran along the foothills. Somehow, I couldn't help feeling that our every move was being watched. After some ten kilometres, we rounded the end of the mountain range, and there, spread out as far as we could see into the heat haze, was the Zambezi Valley - hot, flat, shimmering.

"Where do we go now?" I asked the Int Af guard who had come with us as a guide. The man pointed in the direction of some distant huts.

"We can start there, then we will go from one village to the next. We will find the mealies in the villages."

The trucks eased down the slope, then bumped over ever fainter tracks towards the closest abandoned village. White dust trailed in the air behind us. I noticed the fields on either side were barren and empty, their soils parched and wafer thin. We entered an abandoned village of some twenty huts. Our fingers tapped nervously on the triggers of our rifles. Our driver didn't seem concerned, however. He turned the truck around and reversed up to a small wicker-work hut standing on tall wooden stilts. "Okay!" he shouted.

"What?"

"Bang a hole through that silo, *chef.*"

One of my guys, quicker to work out what had to be done, had already grabbed a nearby shovel. He swung it at the wicker-work side of the hut. A few quick blows broke the brittle sticks, and a torrent of maize kernels poured into the back of our truck. Within a minute we were standing several inches deep in corn seeds, and the wicker silo was empty. The driver crashed the truck into gear, and we lurched off towards the next village.

It was late afternoon by the time we turned and headed back to the PV. The trucks creaked under the weight of maize seed that we had collected, and a steady trickle of grain bled from the sides of the vehicle, splattering the dusty road with creamy specks.

We drove up the rutted track towards the security gate of the PV. The gate was guarded by a sandbagged gun emplacement manned by Internal Affairs soldiers who stood fingering their rifles, their red berets thick with dust. I had never been in a protected village before. I noticed a ramshackle swathe of huts and shacks that stretched beyond the gate and up the hill further than I could see. Built out of bits of sticks, grass, corrugated iron and plastic sheeting, the pathetic homes looked as if they were barely strong enough to hold on to the earth.

At the gate, villagers were being searched. I assumed the guards were looking for food being taken out of the camp to feed terrorists. But looking at the distended bellies of the children in the camp and the hollow faces of their parents, I doubted the peasants had enough for their own mouths, let alone any to spare.

A sullen crowd of peasants gathered around. Our driver crashed the gears one last time, and stopped. He climbed down from the cab, strolled round to the back of the truck and banged down the tailgate. A waterfall of grain poured out onto the red dirt. A stick thin peasant, recently evicted from his home in the Zambezi Valley and now dumped in this hell hole, gazed numbly at me – I realised that to him this crude demonstration of government welfare was just one more insult inflicted in a life filled with despair. The crowd stood watching silently. Old men, haggard mothers, snotty-faced pot-bellied children. How they would share out the grain, I had no idea. How they would survive on this meagre supply until the next harvest, over six months away, I didn't even want to think about.

To get away from the depressing scene, I decided to seek out the District Commissioner. I found him in the only brick building in the camp, fifty metres from the gate. To my surprise, the DC turned out to be Charles Guerney, whom I remembered as a fellow pupil at Churchill High School. Charles shook my hand warmly and made us sweet tea in chipped enamel mugs. Flies buzzed against the grimy window panes as we talked about the war. I asked him how he thought the peasants would survive, now that they were living more than a day's walk from their traditional fields. Charles scratched at an insect bite on his arm, but didn't answer. His gaze turned to the end-of-the-world nightmare scenes beyond the window. He and I both knew events were now moving too fast for us to make a difference. "Look at it," he gestured. "Thousands of people, straight out of the *shateen,* all just dumped here in the last two weeks. The only food they have are those mealies you brought in. I've got a handful of guards with which I'm supposed to control this place. It's impossible. The *gooks* come right in to the camp at night, and threaten the villagers, and I don't even hear about it until the next day. And out there...," he pointed towards the valley, "they are sometimes in groups fifty strong. A few weeks ago an army stick got surrounded. It was touch and go. They only got out when the air-force brought a Hawker Hunter in to provide air cover."

The sinking sun was throwing red and orange spears through the dusty window. Soon it would be dark, and the terrorists would have their reign of the night. I didn't envy Charles, stuck in this place night after night, the only white man here, counting the hours until he had to rise and face another day of the same hopelessness and tragedy.

"Time I left," I said, apologetically.

As we drove down the hill away from the PV and its scenes of human despair, the young DC's last words echoed in my head - "You be careful out there, this *hondo*, this war, is no joke any more."

26 On Patrol

"We have just 'acquired' an informer," the major was saying. "This *gook* was captured a few weeks ago. He's been interrogated by Special Branch and has agreed to provide *int* on ZANLA forces in this area. This *gook*, ex-*gook* I should say, knows this part of the Valley well - it's where he was operating before he switched sides. He also says he knows where the *terrs* have set up a base camp. This guy will be attached to your platoon, and you will use him to find and destroy their base camp."

"Yes, sir," I replied. "Does he carry a weapon?"

"No weapon," replied the major, looking at me. We both understood. Even if you could trust a turned *gondie* not to put a bullet in your back deliberately (and you couldn't), there was no guarantee, with their poor training and even worse discipline, that he wouldn't put one in your back accidentally.

Outside, I met our "guide". I took an instant dislike to Machado. Dressed in brown overalls, he exuded a sly air. He looked about twenty years old. He claimed to speak only Shona and Portuguese, and so would only address me through an interpreter, seeming to relish the convoluted performance this entailed.

Our patrol slipped out of base camp and took a route directly over the mountains to escape detection. We pressed on throughout the day, enduring vicious thorns and crawling through scowling riverbank forests where tsetse flies sucked our blood. The heat was torturous. Although it was only August, at an elevation less than 300 metres, the Zambezi valley already sizzled and hummed with the approach of summer. Adding to our woes, my men had only two one-litre water bottles each - for some reason the army never seemed to have enough water bottles.

It was six o'clock and almost dark when we halted. I summoned George and issued my instructions for our first night-stop. "George, get the guys to split into pairs, and then deploy them in a defensive circle, about fifty metres out, okay? Let me know when it's done."

"Sure thing" said George, and he disappeared into the gloom. I glimpsed his shadowy figure occasionally, as he organised the troops into a widespread defensive ring, just as we had been taught.

Gradually it got darker and darker, until at last I could not make out any of my men. A fiery-necked nightjar started calling– *good Lord deliver us* – and a Scops owl purred softly in the distance. The African sky became an endless black dome, sprinkled with glittering stars. There was no moon, but the starlight was bright enough to cast shadows that pooled furtively under the trees. Scratching noises – small rodents perhaps – emanated from the shadows, making me jumpy. My mind started to run off on its own. I imagined that somewhere out in that gloom the *terrs* were also settling down for the night. How would we find them? Would they find us first? Under cover of darkness, were they already closing in? A small bubble of panic began to well up in my gut. We had camped in a small clearing. Were we too exposed here? Should we move into thicker cover...?

Then I realised that already something seemed to be going wrong. Two figures were emerging out of the gloom. It was George, whispering animatedly with Corporal Ushe.

"What's wrong?" I snapped.

"You tell him, Ushe."

The corporal stiffened awkwardly, then addressed me directly. "Sir, the guys say they don't like the way we have spread out for the night. We haven't been taught to do it like this."

"Well, that's the way we're supposed to do it. It's a standard defensive circle."

The corporal took a deep breath. Faced with a white officer, he needed to choose his words carefully. *Murungus* had a reputation for being quick to anger. "Yes sir, but I'm thinking that that one is only for conventional warfare. When we are on the anti-terrorist patrol we use another way."

What other way was he talking about? I thought back to the last months of our training. I recalled an officer telling us, "We're moving into a phase of classical warfare. The enemy now have tanks, and mortars. We are preparing you to face a full-on conventional assault." I looked out into the inky darkness. Ushe was right. This was no conventional war, not yet anyway. There was no front line here. We had no idea where the enemy was. They could be miles away, or they could just as easily be right behind us, right now.

"Sir?" I sensed fear and urgency in Ushe's voice. I realised then that he was scared that my inexperience could get him killed. The sudden appreciation of my responsibility was overwhelming. I took a deep breath, and tried to think.

Finally I replied, "Okay, Ushe. What do you suggest?"

I sensed the corporal relax, could feel the tension go out of the air between us. Now his voice was easier, more confident - "Sir, the way it is now, any terrorist can slip in between our men in this darkness. If there is a contact, our guys could end up shooting each other. Better we bring all our guys into a close circle, like…like a fist. We face outwards, and we know we are all next to each other. Then, if we see Charlie Tango coming, it is better for you to give your orders. This way, we can talk to each other with our hands. And, sir, like the fist, we can punch this enemy hard, one time."

I knew immediately that the young black corporal was right – and I admired how he had sold the idea to me without a hint of disrespect. George had been right – Ushe was okay.

"Okay, guys, let's do it."

Early the next morning the guide Machado directed us to an area that we had not covered before. It comprised a large forest. It looked promising. We began a sweep of the forest in extended formation. We walked for thirty minutes, then stopped. I waited for the interpreter to translate.

"He says he's not sure. Thinks we'd better go that way."

We walked a little longer, then stopped again.

"He says it's not here. We have to go further north."

I was starting to lose it. The guide was either deliberately wasting our time, or he had no knowledge of a terrorist camp in the area at all. I beckoned him over to me, and signalled George to join us.

"Where is this camp?" I asked Machado. He gave a nervous laugh, and turned to the interpreter. "It's no bloody joke, you slime-ball," I fumed, waiting for the translation.

"He says he thinks it is over that hill."

"Jesus!" I exploded. "Then what the fuck are we doing here?" I spun back to face the guide. "Listen," I hissed, "if you don't take us to the *gandanga* camp right now, I'll fucking slot you right here, okay?" I waved the barrel of my rifle in front of his face. There was no need for translation this time. "George," I seethed, "I've had this bastard in chunks. He's just stuffing us around now."

"I know, I know. Just give me three minutes alone with him," George responded, grabbing the man by the arm. "I'll make him talk."

"Anything," I spat. "Just get the shithead away from me."

I sat down under a tree, and slowly my temper subsided. Minutes passed. I started to wonder what George was up to. George was easily capable of knocking a few teeth out of the *gook* to get him to talk. But I didn't want things to get out of hand. Out here, I realised, a man's life, a black man's life, simply depended on someone else's whim. A few minutes ago, I was so mad I might have gone too far myself. If I had, I would undoubtedly have got away with it; my own troops would have remained mute, and when the disappearance of the guide came to light back at army HQ, it would scarcely have raised an eyebrow. It would have been just one more unremarkable incident in a dirty little war where such things happened all the time.

My macabre reverie was interrupted by George's return. Fortunately, Machado, who was still with him, appeared to be in one piece. "He'll take us there now," George confidently announced. I didn't ask any further questions. I really didn't want to know what had happened between them.

We headed north, my men in an arrowhead formation, the guide at the apex, the translator and myself just behind him. Half an hour later I got a whispered message: "He says the camp is just ahead."

I waved my men into formation, and we started a sweep through. I was keyed up now, eyes peeled for a sign of anything: a hole in the ground, a shelter, a rifle barrel. There wasn't a lot of bush to cover our advance, so I made my guys jog. We ran for five minutes. Tree trunks flashed past - I felt as if I was in some sort of dream, where the scenery moved, but I stayed in one place. I could hear the sound of water sloshing inside the water-bottle on my belt, and the rasp of my breath. I glanced sideways at the sweep of my men. They were keeping up, doing well. My heart began to hammer in my chest, my breath hissing between my teeth. God, please don't let the *Charlies* see us coming...

Then all of a sudden we were out the forest and into open fields. I stopped, stunned. What the..!? There was a low whistle from behind me. I turned around - someone *had* found something. They were pointing to the ground. I walked across to see what it was. There, in the dust, were a few tins, already starting to rust, the ashes of an old fire, and a group of rotten bush shelters. So, there had been a camp here - once. But it had been abandoned weeks, probably months ago.

"Bring that *gook* here," I hissed.

They dragged Machado, panting and heaving, and threw him down in front of me. He was jabbering something in Portuguese. I looked at the snivelling wretch, then kicked him full in the face.

27 Burning the Village

Our patrols lasted ten days at a stretch. We moved from one gaunt village to the next. All were deserted, lifeless. What we were looking for was signs of recent terrorist activity. One morning we crossed a set of fresh footprints in the damp morning dust. Judging by the size, it was probably the print of a ten year old child. "*Mujiba*," Ushe said. "Gone to warn the terrorists that the army is here."

I scanned the valley with binoculars. The endless scrub bled into a grey haze that fused with the pale sky, but nothing moved except a vulture circling a shimmering thermal. "Where the fuck *are* they?" I muttered.

We trudged on. The abandoned peasants' fields beckoned with paw-paws, cucumbers and tomatoes; we picked them to spice up our diet of dry biscuits and corned beef. Along the dusty, crumbling river banks we found dark recesses of shade and squatted through the heat of the day beneath big leafy tamarind trees. Closer to the foot of the mountains, we discovered secret springs hidden in thick groves where trickles of cool crystal water spilled into inviting blue-black pools.

In tribal areas that I had visited elsewhere in the country, peasant farmers erected their huts along roads and tracks like beads on a string, with only five or six huts in a family group. But here in the Zambezi Valley, without the influence of modern roads, a tradition of bigger settlements had survived. Here the villages were commonly made up of thirty or more huts, with the next village several kilometres distant. Such large groupings, I thought, must lend themselves well to social occasions. When there was a beer-drink or a dance, a whole village could join in the hypnotic chant of the drums. For a moment I envied the life these people must have led...a life which the war had now destroyed.

I found myself standing outside a small quiet hut, on the fringe of just such a village. I bent down, pushing the crude wooden door ajar. Dust trickled from the roof. Gloom seemed to spill out from the doorway. I stepped inside, my eyes struggling to adjust to the poor light. The unmistakable sickly-sweet smell of death writhed on the disturbed air, cloying like glue in my throat. A spear of sunlight poked through the thinning, grey thatch and stabbed the opposite wall.

On the floor in front of me was a body.

At first I thought it was a child. But then I realised it was an old woman - shrivelled, shrunken, her flesh almost mummified by the dry heat. She was curled up, as if asleep. She must have been dead for days, weeks. Probably starved to death, unable to fend for herself, after the rest of the village had been forcibly evacuated.

I stared at the body for a few moments, wondering what to do. My training flashed a warning - *booby trap.* Maybe not, but I decided not to move anything, just in case. There was nothing I could do here, anyway. I shut my eyes for a few seconds, some involuntary gesture of respect, perhaps. The incredible, poignant loneliness of the scene refused to go away, dancing mockingly inside my head. *Try and get rid of this*, it was saying. I groped my way back outside, pulling the door shut behind me.

Later that day, we came across a village of some twenty-five huts. We made a precautionary sweep through in extended formation, but like all the other villages we had been through, this one too was deserted. But, unlike other villages, and probably because of its remote location, the army had not retrieved its grain stocks. The wicker silos perched on stilts were still full of maize kernels, a significant food cache for any terrorists who might come across it.

I radioed back to base camp and got approval to burn the village. My men, meanwhile, were picking through the huts, pocketing the occasional trinket. Over the weeks, I too had gathered a significant collection of beads and axes from these kraals. I thought they would make great conversation pieces on my lounge wall back home. Keen to see if there was anything worth filching before I set the place alight, I stepped inside the doorway of the nearest hut.

In the cool gloom inside the hut, I could see a sleeping area covered with blankets. To the side were photographs, plates and cups arranged on a rickety wooden dresser. On the opposite side, on a small table, was an old-fashioned Singer sewing machine, cotton still in the reel. An ancient phonograph stood proudly next to it, complete with a huge fluted brass horn. It was the last thing I expected to see in such a remote corner of the country. The hut had obviously been evacuated in a hurry; everything was just as it had been left, waiting for its owners to return. A beautifully carved axe caught my attention, and I picked it up. Several strings of beads and a copper bracelet were wrapped around the shaft. It had obvious cultural importance, and I decided to save it. Holding onto the axe, I stepped outside again. "Okay guys," I called, "Let's burn this lot."

My men began setting fire to the thatch on the other huts. I pulled a box of matches from my pocket, lit one, and carefully applied it to the grass roof of the hut I had just exited. A wisp of blue smoke, and the tinder dry thatch caught easily. Crackling and popping, the flame grew hungrily, and within seconds the roof was a sheet of fire. I stepped back from the sudden heat, and as I did so, a mangy yellow dog skittered out the hut's doorway. It was a female, heavy with milk. It stopped a few yards away, and looked back, whining. Why hadn't I seen the dog when I was in the hut, I wondered? Perhaps it had been under the bed. And then, as the flames from the thatch roared into the sky, and the sticks of the walls started cracking, I heard a high-pitched crying coming from inside the inferno. The female dog was now running frantically from side to side, looking towards the burning building.

"Jesus Christ!" I shouted, as I realised the terrible reality of what was happening.

My men had all frozen at the first yelps of the puppies. But it was too late. There was nothing we could do to help; the flames were already too fierce. Now all we could do was wait, listening as the terrible cries pierced our very souls, agonising over what we had done. Finally, the roof of the burning hut collapsed, and the pitiful cries from inside fell silent.

28 Mortar attack

Apart from the one set of footprints we had found, we saw no signs of human activity. The valley floor was hot, quiet, and empty. We patrolled as far as the minefield on the Mozambique border, then back to the foot of the escarpment. The only things moving were birds, small groups of kudu antelope, and some stray cattle. This war didn't seem to be a real war, at least not for us. The only thing that was hotting up was the weather. At last the day for our uplift came. We trudged back to the road and rendezvoused with the trucks that had been sent to fetch us.

As I climbed up next to the driver, he broke the news: "Base camp got *revved.*"

"You're kidding?"

"Mortar attack."

I couldn't believe it. While we had been traipsing all over the bush, the guerrillas had taken the fight to our base camp on the other side of the mountains. It certainly confirmed that the war was alive and well in our corner of the country.

"Anyone hurt?"

"We took a direct hit in one of our trenches. Two guys from engineers seriously wounded."

"Casevaced?"

"Salisbury said there were no choppers. Told us to drive them out. But I reckon it was because they were Africans."

"'Cos they're black? That's bullshit."

"Yup."

There appeared to be nothing more to say.

29 Ambush

We were heading for the valley floor again. We rode in three armour-protected troop carriers. I was in the lead vehicle.

Our driver was hopeless. To start with, he was too short to see properly out of the small bullet proof windscreen. He also had some sort of head injury which seemed to have affected his eyesight and ability to judge distance - he hit bumps at speed, and he twice stalled the vehicle. I was just trying to think of a new swear word I could direct at him, when there was a deafening explosion from under our left rear wheel.

"BADAAAM!!"

The truck shuddered, as if mortally wounded.

"Go! Go! Go!" I screamed. The driver panicked and stalled the engine. A ringing silence hung in the air. Debris dusted down on us.

We all suddenly realised the danger we were in, sitting ducks in an ambush. A rippling crackle of gunfire erupted as we feverishly sprayed the roadside bushes with hot lead. A second later there was a flash of red flame behind us, and the third truck in our convoy lurched drunkenly off the road. More rock and dust rained down.

Standard procedure says to get out of a killing zone as fast as possible, but with our front and rear vehicles both crippled, we were going nowhere. Gunfire was now pouring from all three vehicles. Blue smoke drifted in front of my eyes. Fear danced a jig in front of my face. I wondered if I was going to die where I sat.

Fortunately, after a few seconds, I realised that there was no incoming fire.

"Stop firing! Stop firing!" I shouted to my men. I didn't want them to use all their ammo. Gradually they all stopped firing. The last echoes of gunfire bounced back from the mountain, and silence engulfed us again.

Thank fuck it hadn't been an ambush after all. We had hit two landmines simultaneously, but no-one had pressed home the advantage against us.

"Right, get out the vehicles, but walk in the tyre tracks." There was still a danger of anti-personnel mines placed in the road to catch disembarking troops.

Once we were safely out of the vehicles and in defensive positions, I got on the radio. "Romeo, Romeo, One Golf." I needed to raise the RDR relay station which was somewhere on top of the mountain that loomed above us. Without the relay I wouldn't be able to get a message to base camp advising them of the incident.

"Romeo, Romeo, One Golf," I repeated, trying to keep the post-explosion tremor out of my voice.

The radio squawked and hissed. Finally, a crackled response: "One Golf, this is Romeo. Read you three's. Go ahead, over."

I briefly explained our situation and asked for a recovery team, then we settled down to wait.

After a while, someone announced he could see figures moving high up on the side of the mountain. Taking up my binoculars, I scanned the jumble of grey-brown rocks high above us. I spotted three small figures squatting on the rocks high up, watching us. They were carrying rifles.

"Think those are *gooks?*" I asked George.

"Yah. They're probably the ones who put these mines here, and now they're watching what we do next. Let's give them a *rev* with the M.A.G."

The machine gunner cocked his weapon, and fired a few bursts. The distant figures were out of effective range, but realising they had been spotted they melted away into the laughing red-grey rocks and teasing shadows of the mountain.

Eventually, the recovery party and the engineers arrived, a mine detecting vehicle in the lead.

"Now they decide to use the *pookie*. A bit late for that."

The engineer came across to my vehicle and examined the damage. The mine had destroyed the wheel hub. "It wasn't boosted," he commented. "Which is just as well, otherwise you guys wouldn't be looking so happy."

Leaving the recovery team to their work, I told my men we would be going the rest of the way on foot. "It's an extra ten kays," I said, "but until they've cleared the rest of the road there won't be any more trucks going our way." The sun was already sinking behind the mountains. Bundling our rucksacks back on our shoulders, we set off into the last of the afternoon heat, wondering what the valley would throw at us next.

30 A Kill

We covered a lot of ground over the next two days. I had a goal in mind. My map showed there was an abandoned PV far to our north. Purple printing on the map identified the old PV as "Bandima". Even in broad daylight, it had an ominous ring to it. I decided to see what was there. Some instinct told me I would find something.

When we finally arrived at Bandima, however, I was disappointed. The place was a ruin, and the bush had started to reclaim it. The perimeter embankment was already covered by short yellow grass, and there was no sign of the original security fence. Only a few broken pots and termite eaten stumps betrayed the fact that this had once been "home" to thousands of forcibly displaced peasants. It seemed a god-forsaken spot - hardly any trees, thin white soil, stunted bushes. I wondered what sadness now lay underneath the thin cover of gently waving grass.

It was early morning, with just a hint of winter's crispness still in the air. The sort of morning which, a few years before, might have found me cruising a river with friends, looking for an early bite from a tiger-fish. Or the sort of still, cool morning which was perfect for a game drive. But now, with the war, such innocent pursuits had slipped into the background of our lives. Instead, here I was, gazing at the handiwork of a nation tearing itself apart and our morning hunt was now for a far more deadly prey than tiger fish.

The deserted PV made me think of my friend Tony, the guy that I had bottled with the demijohn of wine at university. I remember Tony telling me that he had done his original national service with Internal Affairs, and that every university vacation thereafter he was compelled to do call-up stints in some remote PV. I could now start to imagine what it must have been like out here for him. He probably would have been the only white person within fifty kilometres, and apart from the supervision of PV guard duties, he would have had nothing to do but sit out the endless frustrating days waiting for his "vacation" to finish.

The disconnect between those posted to the sharp end of the war, and those like me who had enjoyed an almost normal life in the towns, had always been this stark. The soldiers serving in the bush faced alternating boredom and death every day, while their luckier townsfolk continued to enjoy all the fun of a busy city social life. No wonder Tony had reacted so violently to the careless remarks I had made during my carefree days at university.

Tony. That was then.

Bandima. This was now.

Am I you now, Tony, I thought to myself? *Years of war? Years of war to come?* I remembered a poster which my brother had back home which read, *What will we do with our Saturday afternoons when the war is over?*

"Over. This might never be over," I muttered.

"Sorry, sir?" enquired the soldier standing next to me.

"Nothing. Just talking to myself."

We were still standing next to the crumbling dirt embankment of the PV. I gazed around, scanning the distant haze. More endless, flat nothing, just cicadas singing in the distant trees, and hornbills looping from branch to branch. There was nothing here. Nothing to see….

But incredibly, there was. Perhaps a kilometre away across the empty plain, I spotted a line of figures walking towards us. I lifted my binoculars. It was hard to tell who they were. Surely they must be soldiers? I could make out what looked like rifles. But who? Why here? I squinted through the binoculars again. The way they were walking in single file, bunched together, rifles slung carelessly over their backs..... No, our soldiers didn't patrol like that! I looked around at my men. I had a stick of six with me. The others were with George and Ushe, a hundred metres further back.

"Get down, quick!" I whispered. "*Charlie Tango!*" I gave the thumbs-down sign for "enemy".

I hurriedly alerted George on the radio, telling him to get his men under cover. A few seconds later I saw them scurrying into hiding behind the embankment.

I lifted my head above the grass again. The figures were still walking towards us. I was sure I could make out a rocket launcher now. They hadn't seen us. I spoke urgently into the radio again.

"Break! Break! Attention all call-signs. This is One Golf. If you can hear this, and you are walking, you must stop now! You are walking into our ambush!"

Only a hiss of static.

I repeated the warning. "Attention all call-signs! You are walking into my ambush. Stop walking now!"

The figures out on the plain trudged on. These were definitely terrorists, then. It was incredible. We were on an open plain. It was midday. We had two perfectly concealed positions to fire from, and the enemy were walking straight into our killing ground.

"Hotel, Golf. Hold your fire until they are really close." My heart was pounding in my ears. My hands shaking.

Safety off.

I sighted down the barrel.

A hundred metres....

There were six of them, walking in single file. They were all carrying AK-47 rifles, except for the one with the RPG rocket launcher.

Ninety...

Eighty...

Now I could see their clothes - jeans and T-shirts, some with bandanas wound around their heads.

Seventy metres....

I was scarcely breathing.

I sighted down the barrel, lining the cross hairs on the first man. Just twenty more steps....

Suddenly, a shot!

It came from my left. Damn it, it was too soon! But it was done now - a fusillade of firing erupted from our two positions. I saw the front terrorist spin round and fall. Even before he had hit the ground, the others were jumping and running and ducking away like startled impala in full flight. Men running for their lives. They ran and ran. Over the far embankment they ran and ran, and then they were out of sight. What a fuck up.

"One Hotel, this is One Golf. Stop your firing!" I realised I hadn't even bothered to shoot.

"Sorry about that," George's voice crackled in my ear. "One of my guys panicked and fired too soon."

"Come across to my position, fast. Make sure all your weapons are on safety." We didn't need any more mistakes.

A minute later the platoon was reunited. I quickly spread the men out into an extended sweep line. We might as well make an effort, in case we had wounded someone.

"Okay," I shouted, "Forward!"

I saw the body of the first terrorist lying on the ground ahead. I put another bullet through it, just in case, then approached. The body was a sickening mess. He must have taken every shot fired in our first volley. The others probably didn't get hit at all. Fuck, fuck, fuck.

"Leave it," I told the nearest soldier. He looked like he was about to vomit.

I raised my voice. "We're going to chase them, okay. We're going to run. Stay in extended line. Machine-gunner, I want you to clear all the thick bush we come across."

We set off at a trot. It was open country, with a few scattered clumps of bush, so it was easy going. We picked up their spoor quickly - it was a scatter of footprints in the sand, all running, all heading the same way.

"They're running for the minefield," I shouted. "Speed it up! *Checha, checha!*"

As we ran, we cleared clumps of bushes in front of us with bursts of quick gunfire. But I wasn't expecting the *terrs* to stand and fight. From the amount of gunfire they had heard, they knew we were a strong group. I was sure they were running, spooked, for the safety of the border.

After half an hour of steady jogging, I glimpsed the metallic glint of the border minefield fence ahead. This could be dangerous, because if the *terrs* couldn't get through the minefield, they might have to stop and fight. Also the bush was a lot thicker here - they could be hiding anywhere. I signalled my men to slow down. They were pretty exhausted anyway, but to their credit they were managing to keep in formation. Now we moved forward cautiously, silently.

I approached a thick clump of trees. I couldn't see through. I entered the bushes slowly. I was shitting myself now. To my left, I glimpsed one of my soldiers inching his way round the outside of the clump. There was another soldier somewhere to my right. A tangle of creepers got round my rifle barrel. I was almost halted by the thick creepers. I leaned down on my rifle to push through...

Suddenly, there was an explosion of leaves a metre in front of me! A blur of brown. I pumped one, two, three quick shots in reflex action. Bang! Bang! Bang! Something brown broke cover, jinking, weaving. Then it was gone.

A duiker! A small buck. That's all. The relief was overwhelming.

I pushed through the last of the bushes. The minefield fence was directly in front of me. The fence was broken and sagging and I could see a well-worn footpath crossing the minefield just beyond. Fresh footprints in the dust mocked us, pointing towards Mozambique and safety beyond.

"Bloody useless minefield!" I cursed, wiping away sweat and camouflage paint from my eyes. "What shit-head thought up this crap!?" My hands were sweating and shaking with adrenalin. I wanted to lash out at someone, everyone: the terrs; the army; the politicians. My impotence made me rage. I wanted to curse the hopeless strategists who had brought us to this mess; I wanted to scream at an enemy that played hide-and-seek.

After a long while I calmed down, began to breathe more deeply. Ushe came across to me. "Sir, there is no more to do here. The men have rested, I think we can go now." I scanned the shimmering bush beyond the minefield once more with my binoculars. Everything looked so peaceful – the grey-green of the distant trees, the occasional swoop of a hornbill, the distant cooing of a dove. Now, I realised, I was secretly relieved our mad chase was over. The terrorists were safe in Mozambique, but we were also safe. There was a lot to be said for keeping that balance.

  "You're right, Ushe, let's go and find a spot to have lunch."

31 Explosion

We had been on back-to-back patrols in the ever-increasing heat for six weeks now. Each ten-day patrol was rewarded with one night's rest and re-supply in base camp, then were sent out again.

When we patrolled, we were always on alert, twenty-four seven. We knew the *gooks* were out there, and they too knew we were there. To reduce the odds of being caught by surprise by the enemy we were always changing our location, changing the pattern of our movements, altering our routine. We never slept in the same place twice, never returned to a waterhole we had already used, never talked above a whisper, never used soap or toothpaste, hardly ever removed our boots. We were always on edge. Now the strain was taking its toll, both mentally and physically. My men's reactions were slowing. They trudged with their heads down, were slower to respond to visual signals, were thinking of their families. We were all simply worn out, and we desperately needed leave.

We were eating our evening meal in the cover of some thick *mopane* forest. Sitting in pairs, we faced outwards, taking it in turns to eat, never talking above a whisper, half the platoon on watch. Our training had been thorough in this regard, but now it was more the knowledge that the terrorists were definitely out there somewhere, anywhere, that kept us alert and quiet. Dusk and dawn were always traditional times for an attack.

I was just brewing a mug of tea on my small gas cooker when it came:

"DOOOMP!" The sound was of a single, distant mortar bomb launching out of its tube. We froze. Arching high into the sky, perhaps a kilometre above us, we had maybe ten seconds. Was it aimed at us? I crouched down. Fear sent prickles up my spine, and icy fingers clawed my gut. There was nothing we could do except count and hope that it didn't land too close... Seven... Eight... Nine....

There was a second explosion. "BOOM."

It was far away. The mortar hadn't landed anywhere close. The *gondies* obviously didn't know where we were. We relaxed.

It had been the same every evening for the past week - at sunset, a single mortar was fired from somewhere on the distant mountains. We assumed it was a signal - someone was watching our movements from the mountains. A single warning mortar fired in the evening meant, "Watch out, security forces in the area".

Night closed in. The *mopane* trees lifted skeletal branches in silhouette against the starry sky. My men quietly shouldered their backpacks, and waited for the order to move. It was our routine - stop for dinner at sunset, then wait for night to fall, then move on under cover of darkness. If anyone launched an attack on our eating place after dark, we wouldn't be there. We would be far away, bedding down somewhere safe.

I stood up, and the men followed my cue without a sound. I led the way - I knew where I wanted to go and it was not hard to walk in the dark once our eyes were adjusted to it. There was no light, no noise, as we moved out of the trees.

We walked for an hour until I found a shadowy grove of tamarind trees next to a dry river bed. The soft sand underfoot would make a comfortable bed. We went down into our defensive circle, packs still on, waiting and listening. The familiar calls of night in the bush drifted over us. Crickets, owls, the distant yelp of a jackal. Still we waited, eyes scanning the confusion of shadows under the trees. There was no sign of movement. No one had followed us. My eyelids grew heavier and heavier...

"Wake up, sir." Someone was whispering and shaking my shoulder. "You are snoring, sir."

"No I'm not," I retorted. I peered at my watch. I had definitely dozed off. My body, exhausted by the endless marching, the heat, and the constant tension of the past weeks, had rebelled.

More minutes passed. Apart from a nightjar burbling *"Good Lord deliver us"* in the distance, there was no other sound.

"Okay, let's sleep," I finally said. I passed my watch to the man on my left. They would do one-hour guard duties, in pairs. When the watch got round the circle back to me, it would be time to stand-to for the breaking dawn. The first time I had used the circulating watch technique, the watch got back to me at midnight - some of the guys hadn't felt like doing their guard shift, and had just wound the watch forward an hour each and passed it on! There had been hell to pay the next morning, and no one had tried that trick again.

I unrolled my sleeping bag, and shaped the still warm sand underneath me into a hollow for my hips. We were a long way from open water, so there would be no mosquitoes to annoy us. The only sound was the shocking acrylic rustle of the army-issue sleeping bags. For God's sake, why couldn't they issue us cotton sleeping-bags?

I climbed into my sleeping bag, boots and all. No ways I wanted to have to wake up in a hurry and start running through the bush without shoes. I felt for my rifle. Its cold steel was reassuringly next to me. A welcome cool breeze tickled my face. I looked up at the stars. The night sky was a confusion of sparkles above me, a dome of distant promise that was at once unreachable, yet beckoning. I picked out Scorpio high above as it pursued Orion across the skies. Sagittarius was there too, bow pulled back. Millions and millions of stars in the wide black sky. It was beautiful and majestic and I felt as if I wanted to fall endlessly into the darkness.

Above: School of Infantry, Gwelo, 1979, Intake 164, army officers' commissioning day. Sgt van Vuuren is third from the left in the front row, and I am fourth from the right in the middle row. George Nolan is first from the left, top row.

Right: 1 Rhodesia Regiment cap badge, and General Service Medal

Below: My brother, Martin, and Ilse, on their wedding day.

A revolutionary propaganda poster which I found while on patrol in the Zambezi Valley. The picture depicts guerrillas holding a 'pungwe' indoctrination session in a rural village.

32 A Smell of Cooking

I woke with a jump. Something burning and meaty assailed my senses, wafting on the night breeze. I could clearly smell it. Some bastard was eating food! Jesus, the *gooks* would pick this smell up from miles away. I stood up and scuttled towards the far side of my circle of sleeping men, picking myself round the reclined humps. I peered at the soldier on watch, but it wasn't him. I crouched down closer to the ground and crawled behind my men, determined to flush out the culprit.

Now there was a faint wood smoke smell, too. Surely someone wasn't cooking after dark? Then I realised the smell wasn't coming from my men at all. It was drifting in on the cool zephyrs of air from further down the hill. Someone, somewhere out there in the darkness, was cooking a meal!

"George!" I whispered fiercely. George was instantly awake.

"George, there's a smell of cooking."

"Yeah, you're right."

"It's coming from out there." My arm swept the darkness. "It must be *gandangas*. I want you to take three guys and go and see if you can find anything. If you locate them, maybe we can give them a *rev*."

"No problem, boss," replied George. I could see his eyes shining. This was just up his street. Within a few minutes, George and his men left, slipping out from our circle. I could see their dark shapes for a few seconds, visible against the pale wash of silver sand, but soon they were swallowed up by the hungry shadows.

It was a long wait. A thin moon rose in the east. A few night birds called. Crickets chirped. Trees crackled and stretched, moths fluttered and bumped. The hissing, twitching, squeaking silence of the African night.

About eleven o'clock, shadowy figures re-appeared. There was a click of safety catches, a whispered password, and George and his team were back. They padded quietly into the circle, and dumped their back-packs.

"Nothing," murmured George as he appeared at my side.

"What do you mean, nothing? They must be out there! How far did you go?" I was as annoyed as I sounded. My pent-up adrenalin was itching for release.

"We must have gone two or three kays," he replied. "We could still smell the cooking most of the way. Then we lost it. We had to come back." He sounded down. I cursed under my breath. There was nothing more we could do until morning. Once more, it looked like we were chasing shadows.

33 Into the Jesse

It was now mid-September, and the temperature was nudging forty degrees in the shade. Brown haze drifted into the valley from distant bushfires. Mopane flies plagued our eyes and ears in their relentless search for moisture. On the valley floor, the endless *jesse* bush shimmered into the distance.

We still hadn't been able to find any sign of the enemy since the day of the kill at Bandima. I set up an OP, an observation post, high on the Mavuradona hills, in the hopes that they would spot some movement in the valley. But day after day, hot, bored and frustrated, the OP radioed in the same report:

"November... Tango... Romeo..." NTR. Nothing to Report.

I decided we should head much further afield, north, into areas of thick *jesse* thorn-bush. We walked for five hours. When we finally reached the *jesse*, I realised the thorny thickets were far too dense for us to move in our usual arrowhead formation. If we wanted to press on, we had no choice but to move in single file. Reluctantly, I signalled my men and we headed forward.

I didn't like the *jesse* at all. In single file with almost no visibility, I knew if we were ambushed it would be almost impossible to counterattack. Nervously I radioed George to keep a hundred metres separation between our sections. At least then, one group could support the other in the event of trouble.

There was no air movement in the thorn-bush. The heat was excruciating, and the cicadas shrilled deafeningly all around. The path meandered to and fro, picking its way desultorily through the thorn bushes. We could see no further than a few metres. As we plodded on, I grew increasingly nervous.

Then abruptly the path opened out onto a patch of cleared fields. George's section was in the lead. They paused, scanned the fields, then spread out and headed across the patch of open ground. They were about fifty metres across the clearing when they came under fire.

Crack! Crack! Crack! Bullets nicked and hummed in the branches above our heads. I heard George's section return fire. Hidden from view by the thorn bushes, my own section crouched down. Then George's voice crackled urgently on the radio, "Golf, Hotel! We're pinned down in the open area ahead of you. I need immediate covering fire!"

Unable to see what was going on in the fire-fight up ahead, I summoned my light mortar. I estimated that George wasn't more than fifty or so metres ahead, so I banged the hand-held tube into the sandy ground and angled the tube towards the sounds of the more distant gunfire. I signalled Ushe to drop in a mortar.

"DOOOMP!" Up went the first bomb.

Silence as the mortar rose in the air, then… nothing.

"What's wrong?"

"No explosion."

Shit! I had forgotten to arm the bomb!

We quickly unlocked the safety caps on the next three mortars, and dropped them down the tube in quick succession. The last one had just launched when there was a gratifying distant explosion, followed by two more. The distant gunfire stopped as suddenly as it had begun. I prayed that George's men were okay, that my mistake hadn't cost anyone their life.

After a few seconds, my radio crackled. It was George's relieved voice. ""Thanks, *china*. They seem to have fucked off." A short while later, George and his men re-joined us.

"OK?"

"Yah, fine." But he looked a bit shocked. He stood clipping fresh rounds into his magazine, avoiding my eye. I didn't press him further – I could see he was dealing with the reality of what had nearly happened.

"You know," George conceded after a long silence, "We'd be well and truly fucked if these *floppies* could shoot straight."

We headed away from the ambush area - it was not the type of ground I wanted to pick a fight in. Our earlier lethargy had, not surprisingly, vanished. We were all acutely aware that we were well and truly in the middle of hostile territory. We knew the terrorists couldn't be far away, and we were conscious of our lack of knowledge of the terrain. I scrutinised my map. We had travelled a day and a half without crossing any water, and my men needed to refill their bottles. A thin blue line on the map indicated a small riverbed a couple of kilometres away. A deserted village nearby was labelled as "Mupapa Kraal". I decided we would head there to dig for water.

It was dusk when we reached the river line, a narrow bed of dry sand squeezed between two steep banks. Scattered along the banks were thick clumps of thorn bushes and buffalo-bean creepers. We followed the edge of the river until, at a sharp bend, we found a way down. In the river bed there was an old hole dug in the sand. The fresh spoor of kudu and smaller buck around the hole suggested there was water not far beneath.

"Dig there." Sure enough, after a few seconds we found muddy but drinkable water. I spread the men out in pairs in a wide, defensive circle, and we took turns to refill our water bottles.

By the time we were nearly finished, the sun had set. Darkness swooped in. I waited impatiently for the last of my men to collect their precious water. The recent contact was still fresh in my mind, and I was jumpy. Strange how some places just give you the creeps - an evolutionary survival sense, perhaps? I crossed to the far side of the river to consult with George.

"Those *gooks* might know about this waterhole."

"Yah. Maybe we could set up an ambush, just on the off-chance?"

"Might as well."

I was just about to creep back to brief my section when I stopped. The hairs were standing upright on my neck.

"Did you hear something?"

"No."

We held our breath, listening. The gathering night-time sounds of the bush whistled and chirped all around us.

"Nothing."

"I could have sworn…." We waited tensely again.

"No, nothing. Must have been one of your guys across the river."

"I'll go and bring them in."

I headed back to gather in my men from their concealed positions on the far side of the waterhole. As I padded across the soft sand, the first stars were beginning to twinkle in the blackness overhead. I could hear the buzzing of crickets and flutter of moths.

Then I heard it again. This time there was no mistaking it. Voices. People talking. The bush seemed suddenly menacing, dark, shadowy.

Shit, shit, shit. It has to be gooks.

I froze to the spot. The voices drew closer. Damn it, we weren't ready for them. And I was caught out in the open.

I sank down and lay as still as I could, hugging the ground. I could feel the warmth of the sand seeping through my shirt, could hear the thump of my heart. I prayed no-one could see me. I lifted my head cautiously, peering into the shadows. The only thing in my favour was the moon had not yet risen.

Then the voices stopped.

Silence. Complete, agonising, endless silence, stretching on and on. The silence of two people trapped in a darkened room, not daring to breathe, each hoping to slip away, but knowing it's impossible to make it to the door undetected.

A sudden shout. "*Hokoyo! Hapana!*" Danger! No! Then the staccato chatter of automatic gunfire. Almost immediately, George's section behind me responded, quick double taps from their FN's at first, then the roar of the MAG. Bullets zipped and whined through the darkness. On the far side of the river, my own section realised what was happening, and also began firing in the direction of the voices. I watched their red tracer carve lines across the sky. Hot lead pinged and hummed all around. It was a blind show of force on both sides. None of us could see our targets - the bush was too thick, and the night too dark.

Then I noticed green enemy tracer starting to come in from my right. The *gooks* must have arrived in two groups. That would explain the shouted warning. I saw a muzzle-flash. I knew we had no men there, so I pulled off a few rounds. My red tracer seared through the darkness.

Suddenly someone kicked my forearm. My whole shoulder shook with the impact. My rifle was knocked from my grip, skittering into the darkness. I looked up to see who had kicked me. There was no-one there. Instantly I knew I had been shot.

I looked down at my arm. It was too dark to see anything, just a black shape against the pale sand. Strangely there was no pain. I willed my fingers to move, but there was no response. Fuck, fuck, fuck!

I rolled onto my left side. My right arm and wrist dragged, dead weight, across the sand, a dark stain trailing behind.

Then a cold, terrible thought – what if there was another bullet coming? What if they could see me lying on the sand? What if I was still in someone's rifle sights? With nowhere to hide, too terrified to move, I felt cold sweaty panic sweep through me. I called out, shakily, "George, I'm hit." I knew he wasn't far away.

"Hit?" I could hear the shock in his voice. Then, "Don't worry. Don't worry." But I *was* worried – death was everywhere around me now. Roaring, stamping, hunting for me, feeling through the bushes, raking the sand, searching for me as I lay quivering in the darkness. It felt as if George, the only person who could save me now, was stuck on the far side of an impassable chasm.

Then I heard George shout, *"White Phos!"* and a second later an explosion of napalm in the bushes lit up the river-bed like day. Splinters of white flame clawed into the dark sky. Branches crackled and popped in the instant firestorm. Shock and awe.

White phosphorous is one of the most frightening things a soldier can face – it burns a hole through anything or anyone it touches, feeding on skin, bone, flesh. The enemy firing stopped immediately. There was a thin chorus of panicked shouts from the darkness, then noises of snapping bushes and running feet. A few seconds later, the bush was silent.

I lifted my head. The stars twinkled, unmoved, above me. A cricket began to chirp again. I managed to croak out, "Thanks, George, I'm coming back." Then I crawled, exhausted, a disbelieving survivor of this sudden terrible maelstrom, back across the white sand, back towards the gentle trees, back to the safety of my comrades.

34 Casevac

The sun rose, carelessly throwing down a morning riot of orange. It had the colour of blood, but the warmth of life. I could feel my heartbeat in my wounded arm, the pulse thin and panicked, but with the end of the long, anxious night, I knew the worst was over.

I scanned the skies for signs of the promised *casevac*. Around eight a.m., the thud-thud of rotors came pulsing through the air, and an Allouette helicopter roared in low over the trees. I could see the gunner leaning out the side, mounted machine gun at the ready. The aircraft hovered as the pilot surveyed the small landing zone that we had marked out with day-glo patches facing the sky. Slowly the chopper descended, kicking up a spray of dust and leaves that whirled around us. George helped me forwards, gently taking the rifle which I was still holding in my left hand. "You won't be needing that in town, *china*," he said. "Have a beer, and say howzit to the chicks for me." Then he turned and walked back towards the trees.

"You okay, buddy?" shouted the gunner above the rising whine of the engine. I threw him a quick glance – bright blue eyes and freckled cheeks in the face of a twenty-year old. Despite his youth, I felt safe, felt I was among family. I nodded. "My first ride in a chopper!" The gunner strapped me into my seat, gave a 'thumbs-up' to the pilot, and a second later, we were lifting up into the air. I turned my attention back to the ground below.

The small landing zone was already falling rapidly away beneath us. I could see my platoon scattered along the edge of the tree-line. The faces of the men were upturned, and some of them held their hands high in silent farewell. Already, they looked like toy figures. The chopper banked to the right, and the soldiers were once again swallowed up in the endless forest.

Now, as we climbed higher, the vastness of the flat, endless grey Zambezi Valley revealed itself to me. I noted familiar landmarks: to the south, the Mavuradona Mountains crouched, guarding the entrance to the valley. Somewhere, dwarfed by the singing silence of those grey hills, was our observation post and the RDR relay station - both would be monitoring my *casevac* on their radios. Beneath me, like a yellow ribbon threading itself across a vast ochre tapestry, was the road we had travelled on when we hit the land-mines. Looking east, I could see the hazy outline of Bandima, where we had ambushed the terrorists at the old PV, and just beyond that, the rise of a small hill where I had found a revolutionary poster nailed to a tree, and pocketed it as a memento. Beyond that, in the distance, I could see the spider-web glint of the border fence and the blurred hazy-blue, flattened expanse of Mozambique.

"This is a lot faster than walking!" I shouted at the gunner, above the roar of the rotors. "And a lot safer."

"Buddy, you're well out of that shit," the gunner shouted back. "No sense in getting yourself killed at this stage. The fuckin' politicians are back in London negotiating a ceasefire, as we speak."

"Really?"

"Ya. Lancaster House conference. Looks like this war is just about over."

I looked back down at the familiar landscape unfurling below. I thought of the weeks I had spent trudging over that sun-hammered red ground. Once, it had seemed to me the right thing to do, to fight for my country against an enemy whose Marxist ideology spurned democracy and whose methods embraced terror. But I realised that now my existence in the war had lost its broader meaning – that with the escalation of fighting and the hardening of hearts that came with it, there was no longer time left for debate, understanding, or compromise. Instead, every hour in the bush had now become simply a matter of brute survival - hunting for water, sleeping rough, hiding from the enemy, trying to stay alive. Kill or be killed had become our overriding motto.

Now, as the chopper roared its easy dominance over the scarred land and lives beneath us, my injured arm began to throb. Awareness, disillusion and pain were my new reality. I realised my days of fighting were over.

35 Ceasefire, 1980

The puppeteers - Britain, South Africa and the Frontline states - once more forced the warring Rhodesian parties back to the negotiating table. With arm-twisting on all sides, everyone reluctantly agreed it was time for a ceasefire and fresh elections.

This time Mugabe contested the election vigorously. Always a brilliant tactician, his formula for winning votes was simple – he used blackmail. Mugabe ordered his guerrillas to fan out across the tribal areas and to deliver a straightforward message to the electorate: *If you don't vote Mugabe in, he'll continue the war.* For millions of rural peasants, weary of being caught up in the crossfire, their lives, families and finances in shreds after years of conflict, their choice couldn't have been clearer.

Almost on the sidelines of the election were the whites. Having abdicated political control a year earlier, the thought that our beloved country might now finally fall into Robert Mugabe's grasp was a horror too frightening for most of us to contemplate. Perhaps out of our growing sense of desperation, rumours begin to circulate. "Did you hear," I was told, "there's a plan for a coup? The Air Force has orders to bomb all the assembly points where the terrorists have gathered. Take the whole of Mugabe's forces out at one go. That's the way to do it!"

Of course! There was no way our army was going to let Mugabe take over. The idea of turning defeat into a stunning military counter-strike at the eleventh hour was comforting. "Things will work out," we said to each other confidently. After fifteen years, hoping for the best had become part of our national psyche.

Indeed, as election day dawned, the army suddenly appeared to be everywhere in the city. Major intersections were manned by soldiers brandishing machine-guns, and armoured cars patrolled the streets. "They're just waiting for the word," was the talk in the bar. With beers poised, we waited for the announcement of the election's final results.

But when the results came on the TV, there was an outburst of cursing.

"What was that?" I asked.

"Bloody Mugabe! He's won."

We were incredulous. The impossible had happened. Muzorewa, the man we had been consistently assured would win, had secured a pathetic three seats. Nkomo had got just twenty. While Mugabe had a land-slide - fifty-seven seats! We watched aghast, but the proof was there on the TV - thousands of cheering Patriotic Front supporters *toyi-toying* and dancing in the streets while Mugabe, the devil himself, proffered a clenched fist in triumph.

As we muttered into our beers, the sound of drums celebrating blew in on the breeze, sending a chill up every spine. For the first time since the days of the 1896 Matabele Rebellion, we whites once more feared for our collective lives. Memories of the Congo rapes flickered behind grim faces. Husbands and fathers, crushed by the reality of their responsibility, slumped speechless at the bar.

Surely now, we said, *the army has to act?* So we waited, expectant, ears peeled for the sounds of the promised coup. But outside the pub, the suburban roads were deserted. There was not a soldier to be seen. The armoured cars had all vanished. The eerie hiatus stretched on into the night, with no sign of the promised revolt. Finally, as morning glimmered on a new horizon and the celebrating drums continued to beat, a slow, grim realisation dawned on us. The coup had been a final bluff, a last puff of conjurer's smoke, luring us into a false sense of security, until it was too late to do anything but watch events unfold. I looked at the drawn, worried faces around me. Everything that our white community had been brought up to believe would never happen, had now happened. People were in disbelief. Sanctions, call up, fifteen years of war, struggle and shortages, 30,000 people dead - what had it all been for? Had we gone through all that, only to be served up an outcome that now seemed the worst possible result?

Amidst the swirling confusion, conspiracy theories abounded. Who sold us out? Was it the British? The South Africans? Or Ian Smith himself?

A few, however, started to ponder if this wasn't perhaps a trap of our own making. The years of strife and discord, could they have been avoided after all? Could we not have got a better deal for ourselves and our children if we had listened to wiser counsel, negotiated earlier, before the war hardened everyone's hearts? Did we fritter away our early advantage, too blinkered to foresee the logical historical outcome of our stubbornness, too selfish to share the privileges we had now lost anyway?

Whatever those answers, it was too late to look for alternatives or lay blame. Life, in the unique privileged form that my grandfather, my father and I had known it, was over. Ninety years of white supremacy had finally evaporated. Now the new Zimbabwe, in all its dancing, chanting reality, lay waiting for us just outside the door.

- Book Two -

Zimbabwe

36 *Pamberi!* – Forward!

The first few weeks after Mugabe came to power held a morbid fascination for us whites. To the beating of drums, the state-run "Voice of Zimbabwe" trumpeted Mugabe's triumph over the "running dogs" of imperialism, and declared that the correct form of address between people should henceforth be the Marxist "Comrade" rather than the western tradition of "Mr" or "Mrs". As the propaganda from the radio became more virulent, we began to fear the worst sort of ethnic reprisals.

But the cues coming from the new government seemed contradictory, if not schizophrenic. While we couldn't ignore the raging rhetoric on the radio, at the same time, as if in a parallel reality, Robert Mugabe now appeared on TV preaching reconciliation between the races. He even went so far as to announce he was retaining Lieutenant General Peter Walls as head of the country's new integrated army, and was appointing white ministers to head key Ministries such as agriculture and commerce.

As we tried to make sense of these contradictions, it seemed to me that there were two voices within the new government, each vying for supremacy. The Marxists, almost juvenile in their ferocity, seemed intent on extinguishing all traces of capitalism and the colonial past. The other, however, was a voice of reconciliation, surprisingly mature and practical, urging reason and consolidation. With no network linking whites into the new black government, it was impossible for us to work out what was really going on. One thing was clear though – we whites, outnumbered fifty to one by blacks, now wielded almost no political power. For the first time in a hundred years, it was black Zimbabweans who would be the mappers of the country's political future.

Under these circumstances, the best we could do was to leave politics to the new government and get on with our own lives. For me, that meant starting a new job and looking for a home where Debby and I could move in together. I searched the classified columns for houses to rent, but with the end of the war had suddenly come an influx of foreign-paid expatriates into the capital city (now re-named Harare) and rents had soared well beyond our reach. Conversely, many whites were now in a hurry to leave the country, and they were putting their houses up for sale at bargain prices. I decided to seize the opportunity and bought one.

92 Enterprise Road was an attractive colonial-style dwelling in the up-market suburb of Highlands. With wide verandas wrapping around two sides and high pressed-steel ceilings inside, it was ideally suited to Harare's sunny climate. The house sat on a lush acre of land, graced by red flowering *erythrina* trees at the front, and rampant bougainvillea, mulberry and banana trees at the rear. A custom-built bar on the east side overlooked a deep blue swimming pool. The whole tropical package came at the knock down price of $29,000.

For young people starting out, it was traditional to share a house. It helped with costs and made for a livelier social atmosphere. I invited two friends, Louise and Joneta, to move in with Debby and myself.

After moving the furniture in, the four of us were sitting in the lounge, relaxing with beers, when our new cook, Taibu, padded in. "Dinner is ready, master," he said.

"Great, thanks Taibu."

"No problem, master."

Debby giggled. "Why does he call you master?"

"I've no idea," I replied huffily. "'Boss' would do." We sat down at the dining table. A tasty roast chicken sizzled on the tray in the middle. "I'll carve."

As we tucked in hungrily to the roast. Joneta raised her wine glass. "A toast," she said, "To our tough life in Africa."

"Agreed," said Debby. She sloshed wine into a crystal goblet. "Pure hell."

Towards the end of the meal, feeling replete and contemplative, I turned to the others. "You know," I said thoughtfully, "we're living in a new society now, so maybe we need to consider changing the traditional master-servant relationship?"

"What *are* you whittering on about?" said Louise, topping up her glass.

"Well, maybe these days we should bring our domestic servants more into our circle. I mean, treat them more as family members rather than just workers."

Debby's wine glass stopped half-way to her mouth. She looked at me suspiciously. "Uh-hum. And...?"

"I mean, maybe we should think of inviting Taibu to join us at the dinner table, instead of him being relegated to the kitchen after he's cooked the meal."

The girls gazed at me as if I had gone completely mad. Joneta coughed and peered intently into her wine, as if an answer to my sudden medical affliction might be found there. For a long time it seemed no-one could find words for a suitably restrained response.

"Graham," said Debby finally, breaking what was now a long, uncomfortable silence, "Whatever it is that you're smoking, I suggest you get off it...fast"

I took the hint, and didn't raise the subject again.

37 The Great Train Robbery

What I had hoped would be the start of a long period of domestic bliss with Debby soon began to fall apart. My girlfriend seemed to be growing increasingly restless, distracted and distant. Eventually, I asked her what was wrong. At first she refused to answer, but when pestered further, in a rare expression of exasperation she exclaimed, "It's just like being married!" There was frustration in her voice - as if she felt we should have something more than just a pleasant life together. I wondered if it had something to do with me. Or was it just because the wartime tension and excitement was now missing from our lives?

A few days later, I returned home after work. There was an ominous quiet in the house. Propped up on the bed was a note. My heart started to pound in my ears. I tore the note open and read it. It made no sense to me. I heard Taibu clattering in the kitchen, and rushed through. "Taibu," I demanded, "where's the madam?"

"Miss Debby gone, master," the old cook replied quietly. "Another madam take her to airport."

"The airport!" Clawing fingers of ice gripped my stomach. A wave of heartache that I'd never felt before swept up from my core. I rushed to the airport, and caught up with her just as she prepared to board a plane. When Debby saw me she was visibly unnerved.

"Oh, Graham, you shouldn't have come here!"

"Why? What are you doing? Where are you going?"

"I'm moving to Jo'burg."

It was the worst possible answer. I felt as if my heart was being ripped out. "Oh, please don't," I begged, "Don't go. I don't want to live without you."

"I have to, Graham. I can't stay with you now." Tears welled in her eyes. "Goodbye, Graham." Then she turned and walked away.

With Debby gone, it seemed to suck the air out of my life. I could hardly breathe, I felt sick and giddy all the time. It had taken me so long to find this girl, now it seemed as though she had suddenly fallen off a cliff in front of me. But it was worse than that, because I still had no answers as to why she had left. Alone in my bed at night I howled with despair at the unfairness of it all. I turned to alcohol to drown my grief. Days blurred into weeks, then into months, and I scarcely functioned. My friends looked on sadly, impotent, unable to assuage my overwhelming sadness.

When the worst of my private grieving and self-pity was done, I turned to the one person who could provide me with the quiet understanding and healing support that I knew I needed.

"Look. Two tickets for Vic Falls," I showed my brother. "I had planned a trip with Debby, but now...."

Martin correctly read the implied call for help. "So now you need someone else to drink with? Okay, I could do with the break."

Which is how we came to be chugging up the Zambezi River on a leaky old boat that the locals referred to as the "Booze Cruise".

"What is your name?" I asked the waiter standing in front of me. Scrawny grey arms, all sinew and veins, drooped by his sides. He was probably less than thirty years old, but a lifetime of hard toil, little food, and repeated bouts

of malaria had clearly taken their toll. His starched white
shirt and shorts were too big for his thin body, and the
baggy shorts were held up by a tightly pulled piece of
string. With grey flecks at his temples, he looked closer to
fifty.

"My name is Temba." A broad smile flashed across
eager-to-please yellow teeth.

"Very good, Temba. This is my brother." I pointed
towards Martin, who merely arched an eyebrow. Martin
always managed to project an air of dignity. "My brother
drinks lots of beer. You will understand what that means,
Temba?"

"Yes sir."

"Okay, I want two beers; a Lion for him, and a
Castle for me, okay?"

"Yes, sir," replied the waiter obediently.

"*Checha!*"

"I am gone, sir." The waiter turned and scampered
down the shaky metal ladder to the rumbling lower deck of
the boat. While we waited for him to return with our beers,
my brother and I looked out across the Zambezi. The river
was wide but it hurried with a sense of purpose past the
boat, as if shaking off the torpor of the day's heat. Small
rapids chuckled and gurgled, playfully flicking drops of
liquid sun in the air. Jagged black rocks broke the surface
here and there, providing a resting place for skimmers and
other water birds. Along the river banks, tall vegetable ivory
palms waved gently at us while the occasional crocodile,
mouth agape, basked in the last of the afternoon sun.
Further away, where the purple shadows crouched among
thick tangles of bushes and vines, shy bushbuck observed
our passing. Overhead, parrots and hornbills swooped,
squawking and hooting. In the distance, the white spray

from the Victoria Falls smoked above the canopy of the rainforest.

There was a clinking of bottles, and the waiter's peppercorn head re-appeared at the top of the stairs. Balancing a steel tray bearing two beers and two tumblers, he gingerly headed towards us. I noticed there were no labels on the beer bottles - a shortage of glue at the brewery, no doubt - so the bottle caps were left balanced on top of the bottles, allowing us to identify which beer was which. We took the drinks and the jam-jar thick tumblers. These days it was best to pour beer into a glass before drinking it. That way you could spot any "floaties" in the beer. (Once I had forgotten, and swigged straight from the bottle, like we used to do in the old days, and I had been rewarded with a dead cockroach in my mouth.)

The waiter turned to go. "Temba," I barked, "I want one Lion, and one Castle."

"Yes sir. This one is Shumba, and this one is Cassel." The old waiter chewed his cracked lips nervously, and pointed at the drinks we were holding. His eyes flicked momentarily towards my brother and his bushy beard. White men with beards were often ex-Selous Scouts, flotsam from the recent war, angry and unpredictable, if not pure crazy, their tempers always on a hair-trigger.

"No, Thomas. Temba. Whatever your name is," I said. "I just want you to fetch us *another* round, okay? You take so bloody long, by the time you get back with more beers, we will have finished these ones. We don't like waiting. Comprendez?" It sounded harsh even to my angry soul, so I softened it by adding, "Just go and bring us more beers. You look after us, maybe you get a big tip, hey?"

"Yes sir. I'm coming *manji-manji*, now-now." The waiter relaxed, now that he knew where this was going. Just keep the beers flowing, then these *marungus* would be happy. He disappeared down the ladder again.

I stared again at the river at it hurried past the boat. The deep ho-ho-ho of a hippo drifted across the warm still air. It was all so beautiful and peaceful, but the magic was lost on me, the pain of losing Debby still too fresh in my mind.

I glanced self-consciously across at my brother. Martin had been silently observing me across the top of his beer glass.

"Cheers," he said, lifting his glass in salute.

"You're a good man, *boet*," I replied gratefully.

"Strange how when we were younger, I couldn't see that." His boisterous, carefree attitude when we were teenagers had irked me no end.

"That was before you learnt how to drink and misbehave."

"And chat up chicks."

"*Yah*, and that. A university education is clearly worth the price."

We both took long swigs of beer.

"It's tough in Africa." Martin leaned back in his deck-chair. Gesturing with his beer at the sunset strutting its stuff across a crimson sky. "All this."

"Shit hard," I agreed, though somewhat half-heartedly. Hurt still throbbed somewhere deep inside.

We listened to the thrum of the boat's engine, and watched the wake drifting behind us in the last rays of the day. The sun, sunk to the horizon, cast a red trail of blood into the distance.

The waiter was back at my side with more beers.

"Ah, the next round! Good man, Temba. Now, *shamwari*, kindly do us the favour of bringing us a further two beers."

We guzzled continuously for the duration of the cruise. The sunset splendour and the alcohol finally worked their spell; my sorrows submerged, at least for the moment. When the boat finally tied up at the jetty, the darkness and humidity of the African night hugging us, I pushed a generous cash tip into the waiter's hand.

"Square now?"

"Square, boss. *Tatenda*"

"*Hazeku indaba.*" No problem.

We were poured into a stuffy, rattling bus, which ferried us back to Victoria Falls town. Bouyed on our alcoholic haze, my bother and I sang a loud mixture of indecent drinking songs, and made rude comments at a couple of grubby Swedish backpackers snogging up front. When the bus finally reached town, we stumbled down the steps.

"Might as well head for the casino," I slurred.

"Right behind you," hiccupped my brother.

We stumbled off in the direction of the casino. Nightjars fluttered across the warm tarmac in front of us, and the distant sound of drums made the warm night air pulse with an ancient rhythm.

As we crossed the railway track which connects Zimbabwe to Zambia, I glanced along the parallel lines of vanishing silver, and saw something glinting deeper in the darkness. I looked again, and could just make out the black bulk of a diesel loco, sitting in a siding.

"Hullo," I commented, "someone's left a train lying around."

"Bit careless in this day and age," replied Martin. "It might get nicked."

We looked at each other.

"We could..."

"....just take a look."

Partly it was the alcohol talking. Mainly it was that I didn't care any more – I just wanted a way to erase any hint of my aching undercurrent of loss, frustration, anger.

"Fuck it, let's do it."

The train turned out to be smaller than we had hoped for, just a maintenance car really. But with roll-down canvas sides it was easy enough to get inside. We clattered into the darkened cab.

"We're in," said Martin. His voice echoed tinnily in the small space.

"Shh, shh," I giggled.

"Let's see if we can start it."

Much fumbling around on the dashboard ensued. "I can't see. We need a light".

"Try the buttons".

We bashed every button on the dashboard. A broad beam of light suddenly surged up the track, washing the trees on either side a ghostly white.

"*Yussus*! Turn it off!"

We killed the headlight. Holding our breath, we strained our eyes up the tracks. Had anyone noticed? We were both thinking about the soldiers patrolling the station platform just a bit further up the track. The Zim army weren't likely to take kindly to a couple of *whiteys* messing around with their government rolling stock in the middle of the night.

But all seemed peaceful. We fiddled with a few more buttons.

"BAAAARP!!" went the hooter suddenly.

"Ha ha ha!" I collapsed in helpless mirth.

"Ssshh!"

"Look," I said, when I had finally recovered my composure, "that must be the ignition." I pointed to a small lock on the dashboard. "We need an ignition key."

There was a pause.

"What are you doing now?"

"Looking for a twenty-cent piece. I can feel wires underneath the lock. If I can just short them out with a coin.....There!" I exclaimed triumphantly. A big red light glowed on the dash. "Now to find the Start button."

We pushed everything again. Headlight. Hooter. All the bells and whistles. And then suddenly, with a splutter, the engine coughed into life.

"Shit! It's going!"

"Sheee-it!"

The engine tone shifted to a throaty rumble. The noise seemed to fill the cab, rattling the roof, vibrating the metal floor.

"Can you make it move?"

We fumbled with more levers and handles. But now vital seconds were ticking away. With the grumble of the motor rolling through the still darkness, we both started to lose our nerve, thoughts turning to the soldiers at the nearby station who would undoubtedly be already on their way to investigate the commotion.

"Mart, we'd better kill it, it's too noisy."

"Affirmative. See if you can find a decompression lever."

We pushed buttons and pulled more levers, but to no avail. The engine kept running. In desperation, I took a handful of wires from beneath the dashboard, and yanked. Still the engine grumbled on.

"Bloody diesel."

"We'd better just leave it and piss off."

"Yah, okay."

We both tumbled awkwardly down the side of the car. Gravel chips scrunched underfoot. Another glance up the line. Did we imagine that we could see distant figures heading towards us? We didn't intend hanging around to find out.

"*Pamberi Mugabe,*" I snickered. Forward Mugabe.

"*Handei.*" Let's go.

"Eat my dust."

And then we were running drunkenly through the darkness, ignoring the thorns that clutched vainly at our legs, laughing and shushing each other, and giggling again with the adrenalin. Up yours, Bob! Victory is ours!

38 A Brush with the Army

The hot air rose in waves off the shimmering tarmac, blowing in through the open window like a blast from an open oven door. The old government pick-up, its broken speedo' stuck on zero, rattled and shook as it negotiated Africa's endemic potholes. Nigel, who was driving, struggled to keep his grip on the juddering steering wheel which seemed to spin with a life of its own. Nigel and I both worked in the Ministry of Housing, he as an architect, I as a town planner. Nigel was taking me to view some buildings that he had designed and built for a pilot housing project.

"The only snag is," said Nigel off-handedly, as we threaded our way through the crowds of people on the streets of Chitungwiza township, "this housing project has been taken over as a temporary army camp."

"You're joking!" I said. Since the Independence Arch on the airport road had been blown up by some disgruntled soul, security had been tightened at all official buildings. Two whites driving into an army camp were, I suspected, hardly likely to be welcomed with open arms. However, it was too late for second thoughts. We were already drawing up in front of a red and white boom gate manned by a slouching soldier.

"*Maskati,*" chirped Nigel to the guard. "*Maswere ere?*" Good day, how are you? The guard scowled, eyeing us sideways, his finger tapping the side of his AK-47. Nigel waved his ID. "Nigel Horrell. From the Ministry of Housing," he added imperiously. The guard approached, studied our ID's, then reluctantly lifted the boom.

We drove through the gate, and soon found the houses Nigel wanted to show me. We parked and got out. We walked through the buildings, Nigel proudly pointing out the economies of his design. "See how easily these houses can be extended by their owners. This has to be the way of the future," he enthused. "Solid and simple, yet very adaptable."

We soon finished our inspection. I glanced out a window, and spotted two soldiers standing near our car. "That's great, Nige, but I'm not keen to hang around here too long. Perhaps we should make a move?"

"OK, no problem." We walked back towards the van. The two soldiers spotted us. From the looks on their faces, I could tell they weren't happy.

"Hey, you, *marungu,* what are you doing here?" one shouted at me as I moved to open my door. I spotted a beer bottle in the man's hand. His shirt was hanging out, and his fly was half open. I ignored the question, simply waving some paperwork importantly in the air and started to climb into the car. The man shouted again.

"Hey, you shit, answer me, why are you here?"

Nigel started to explain. "We're from the Ministry of...."

"Don't you talk to *me!*" the soldier exploded at Nigel. "I not talking you!" Then he swung round to me again. "What fuckin' you here for, hey?"

My blood boiled at his rudeness, but I did my best to keep my cool. "We have permission from the government to look at these houses. We have already shown our permits to the guard on the gate."

"The government!" the man shouted. "Do you know who is the government here? This is not Ian Smith any more!"

I had had enough. Regardless of colour, pissed yobs rank lower than pond scum on my social ladder. "We are leaving now," I said as politely as I could muster. "If you have any problems, you can call the Ministry of Housing."

"Hey, *marungu*," snarled the soldier, "you know what is this one?" He pointed to the officer's pips on his shoulders. Stupidly, I hadn't noticed them before.

"Captain," I replied, trying not to show the concern that suddenly leapt at my throat.

The soldier stepped round the front of the car, staggering slightly, holding himself up with one hand on the bonnet. "Yah, is *Capitain. I* am the officer in charge this camp." He was triumphant now. His alcohol fuelled breath washed over me. "Four years fighting *chimurenga*, now this is my camp."

I realised I had to be careful now. This was an ex-guerrilla, he had none of the respect the old RAR soldiers still showed to us whites. A drunk guerrilla is about as unpredictable and short-fused as a grenade with a loose pin.

"*Mazvita*, thank-you, Captain," I replied, my smile a rictus as I tried to sound pleased, tried not to show my scorn. "We are very glad to meet you. We are inspecting these houses here, for the government." I pointed. "We are doing a report on the condition of these houses, and we will put in our report that you have done a very good job looking after these houses. On behalf of the Ministry of Housing, I would like to thank you *very* much for looking after these buildings so well. You obviously run a very well disciplined camp here."

It was over the top, but fortunately the man seemed too drunk to pick up on the sarcasm, responding instead to the flattery. "Yah," he slurred. "Is very good. Me, I am in charge this one. I am the one for this discipline in the army..." Then he remembered, "But you needing permission to enter! I give you no permission."

I was eager not to go down that track again. "I'm very sorry for that, Captain. The Ministry should have told you we were coming. Anyway, that's okay now, I will put in a good report. We will be leaving immediately." I was already climbing into the car as I continued to babble. Nigel, following my cue, climbed in and started the engine. "Thank-you, sir!" I saluted through the window. Nigel turned the car towards the gate. Suddenly the drunken officer shouted something at the guard on the boom. I held my breath. Nigel waved at the guard. In slow motion, the boom lifted. I heaved a sigh of relief.

"Just as easily, he could have kept it shut," noted Nigel unnecessarily as we accelerated away.

"Nigel," I said, "Don't fucking ever bring me here again."

39 False Dawn

In 1982, just two years after Mugabe's victory, a few hundred disgruntled ex-guerrillas began a minor revolt. All Matabele's, the dissidents felt they were being treated as second-class citizens by the predominantly Shona government. They retreated into the dusty western scrub around Bulawayo, the country's second largest city, and began a series of robberies and skirmishes against government forces.

Mugabe, always paranoid about any form of dissent, responded with over-riding force. He despatched his fearsome Korean-trained Fifth Brigade into Matabeleland. For the Shona soldiers, this was a golden opportunity to get back at their traditional Matabele rivals. The army sealed off Matabeleland, and launched a reign of terror designed to show the locals who was in charge. Twenty thousand Matabele, almost all of them innocent civilians, were slaughtered. Thousands more were raped and tortured. The bodies were buried in unmarked mass graves or thrown down old mine shafts. *Gukurahundi*, they called it – the rains that wash away the chaff. Joshua Nkomo, who fled to Botswana during these dark days, put it bluntly - he described Mugabe's rule as "the worst government in the history of the country".

Rumours about the atrocities soon began to circulate within the white community, but the stories were roundly dismissed by the government as racist smears.

A few brave priests and human rights workers then raised the alarm in the overseas media. *Surely*, they asked of western governments, *you're quick enough to denounce the*

*apartheid regime in South Africa, so you can't let these
worse abuses in Zimbabwe pass without protest, can you?*
But Mugabe's western apologists averted their eyes and
pretended nothing was happening. The official silence
around the world was deafening. This, I believe, was the
moment when Mugabe discovered that he could do anything
and get away with it.

It wasn't much fun in the Ministry of Housing any
more, either. My previous boss, a successful and hard-
working engineer, had fallen victim to the push to replace
experienced white civil servants with more compliant black
lackeys. I soon discovered his replacement was a difficult
customer:

"This housing policy you have written is a policy for
dogs!" the new Director screamed at me, fluttering a clutch
of papers in my face. "You white people think that Africans
must live like animals!" He glared at me, a bead of sweat
running down his nose.

I tried to keep my cool. "Sir, core housing," I
protested, "is the most successful solution to housing
shortages in the Third World. It's a way to provide a small
home for everyone who needs one." I had worked for weeks
on this draft policy. The country urgently needed guidelines
to help it tackle the huge housing backlog, and I was proud
that I had been able to come up with a comprehensive,
practical recommendation so quickly.

The Director scowled at me. "The Minister has
promised to provide the people with four-roomed complete
houses," he spat. "So *that* will be your policy!"

"But the government can only afford to build a few
hundred houses like that," I argued. "What about the rest of
our homeless people? Where will they live? The minister's
promise doesn't make any sense."

The Director rolled his eyes at the ceiling. "Atkins, you don't get it, do you? I don't care about the bloody people. Whatever the Minister wants, that's what we do."

I was so taken aback, I didn't answer immediately. Seeing my stunned silence, the Director adopted a more conciliatory tone. "Listen, Atkins, you are young and idealistic. You want to help people, I understand that, but it's not how things work in the world. I have been in this game in Kenya for the last ten years. Believe me, it's the same here – politicians just want to show off. They want to be on TV and in front of the cameras. Look, I have a posting to the UN ahead of me if I play my cards right, so if the Minister wants gold-plated taps on his houses, that is what I will give him. Understood?"

I understood all too well. I also understood there was no future for me in government service. I tendered my resignation.

Some time later I applied for a lecturing vacancy at the University of Zimbabwe. Invited to an interview, I sat in front of a panel of three who quizzed me politely. I was ideally qualified for the position, but I sensed they were just going through the motions. They said they would be in touch soon, and showed me the door. Sure enough, a rejection letter arrived in the mail a few days later. "You never stood a chance," one of the panellists later confided to me. "We were given a clear brief to find a black person for the job."

40 Drowning our Sorrows

We named the pub in our house "Not the Red Lion" (a parody of the most common UK pub name) and instituted a regular Wednesday night drinking session. "A clean bar is a happy bar," self-appointed barman Rob French quipped, diligently wiping up spilt beer as an enthusiastic tide of patrons played balloon volley-ball across his counter. The neighbours, despairing at the music and noise, complained to the police of our illegal *shebeen* activities, but when a B-car arrived, we simply offered the amused cops a crate of beers and sent them on their way. Inside, our voices remained shrill and our laughter over-sized as we banished beyond the circle of light and merrymaking our worries for the future.

War had helped us hone our ability to make the most of a bad time. Now, marginalised from national politics, subject to reverse racism, and witnessing the clumsy attempts of Mugabe and his lackeys at running the nation, it became de rigueur to "pull the piss" out of the establishment. When a government minister warned "Rhodesians" against celebrating the anniversary of UDI, it was too good a challenge for us to turn down. We sent out dozens of invitations for friends to join us "in colonial dress" for a day of "badminton, cucumber sandwiches and draught beer".

On the day, scores of merry-makers arrived. Soon our driveway was filled with cars, so late-comers were directed to the church car park across the road. The party was a great success. With the extra spice of knowing we were cocking a snoot at the government, everyone made sure they enjoyed themselves.

A group of air-traffic controllers were regular patrons at "Not the Red Lion" and they attained almost cult status for their outrageous drunken exploits. After one drinking session at a city hotel, Alan decided to jump up and down on the roof of a car parked on the street. Police on patrol spotted the disturbance and rushed to make an arrest. "Hold your horshes," slurred Alan, "I believe I can explain everything." He then produced a set of car keys, opened the door of his damaged car, started the engine and drove off.

Another time, in an effort to liven up what threatened to be a dull evening in the public bar of the airport, Alan and a friend doused their heads with whisky, then set fire to themselves. "Look!" said the human torches as they strolled casually round the lounge in front of alarmed patrons, "Perfectly safe. See how the whisky burns, not the hair!" The long suffering Airport Manager, whose patience had worn thin with this sort of exploit, summoned the police in a fit of rage. Two black officers quickly arrived. Unsure as to whether a law had actually been broken, the police then placed Alan in handcuffs in a corner of the bar, and began to question the friend. Bored, Alan looked around and made an interesting discovery: an FN rifle had been left carelessly propped up against the wall by one of the policemen. Gleefully, Alan picked up the rifle between his handcuffed wrists, and strolled back over to the policeman.

"Excuse me, *shamwari*," he interrupted, "is this yours?"

"What now?" muttered the policeman, turning round. His jaw dropped as he found himself staring down the barrel of his own gun. "Put... put that down," he stammered.

"Oh, so this *does* belong to you then?" Alan calmly handed the rifle back to the apoplectic cop. "*Shamwari,*" Alan continued in a fatherly manner, "You need to be more careful. This sort of mistake will not make good reading in your report."

Frustrated with the tensions of life in the city, we took every opportunity to escape into the solitude of the bush. One day, my friend Chris Bradshaw was driving us to Hwange National Park. It had been a slow, tedious journey because of the frequency of police roadblocks. The roadblocks were ostensibly part of a road safety blitz, but their real purpose we knew was to thwart the movement of dissidents and to hamper journalists trying to report on the Matablele uprising. Chris, who was driving, had had enough of the frequent delays. "If one more cop asks me to test my lights, indicators, and hooter, I think I'll have a fit," he muttered darkly. Suddenly, ahead of us, loomed yet one more roadblock. "I'm going to put the whole bloody lot on, this time," Chris spat. He flicked his headlights, switched on the hazard flashers, and leant heavily on his hooter.

As we approached the roadblock our car was a blaze of hooting and flashing lights. The effect was remarkable - a policeman who had been languidly waving us down, suddenly jumped out of the road, snapped to attention, and saluted us. Others slouching around the roadblock, shot bolt upright.

"They think we're a government minister!" I exclaimed with glee. "Go, Chris, go!" However, instead of taking the opportunity to drive right on through the roadblock, Chris slowed to a stop opposite the saluting policeman. Dripping false pleasantry, Chris greeted the cop.

"Morning, my good man. As you can see, everything in my car is working perfectly."

The cop's brow furrowed as he realised he was facing, not a senior government minister, but just a couple of white youths. He dropped his salute. "What do you think you are DOING!?" he demanded.

"I'm just showing you that everything in my car is in perfect working order," replied Chris calmly. "Thought it would save you time."

The policeman was apoplectic with rage. I shrank in my seat, mentally kissing goodbye to our holiday before it had begun.

But we were in luck. After demanding to see Chris' licence, the cop hesitated – you could see the thoughts crashing into each other behind his eyes as he weighed up the pros and cons of making this into a full-blown incident. After all, we clearly weren't dissidents. He buried his forehead in both hands, as if hoping that perhaps this was all a dream.

"Ah, you white peoples...," he muttered finally. "...Just go. Just go."

We sped off down the road, and I heaved a sigh of relief. "Nice one, Chris," I said. "Let's not try *that* again."

The police roadblock is synonymous with Africa. Everyone has a story to tell about them: my friend Jeff told me how he was once heading towards the Copperbelt mining region in Zambia with a group of South African work colleagues. On the outskirts of Lusaka they came across their first roadblock – shiny police car on the side of the road and smartly dressed constables in uniform manning a black and white barrier. After a perfunctory check, they were allowed to proceed. The further they travelled away from Lusaka, however, the less professional the police roadblocks became; shiny police cars gave way first to dusty Landrovers, then to battered pickups, then finally no official vehicles were visible at all; smart police uniforms gradually morphed into tattered camouflage fatigues then into motley assortments of jeans and headscarves. After two hundred kilometres, the well-spoken policemen of Lusaka were a distant memory, replaced by suspect drunks and gun-wielding militia.

Nearing their destination, Jeff spotted another battered oil-drum in the middle of the road, beside which a rag-tag group of gun-toting individuals slouched. Standing next to the drum, a black woman wearing a police cap was gesticulating wildly. Confused, Jeff brought the vehicle to a halt. The policewoman continued to wave wildly. Jeff glanced nervously at her, lifting his palms upwards as if to say "What now?" The woman stalked impatiently towards the car, and thrust her head inside the window.

"Hey, driver, what colour am I?" she demanded.

Taken aback, Jeff didn't know what to answer. Clearly this was a sensitive question, requiring an unusual degree of tact. "Er, um, well," he finally ventured, "I guess you are … er… a light shade of tan."

"No, no, stupid!" shouted the woman, now even more agitated. "What colour am I?" she repeated.

Choking back his incredulity, Jeff glanced at his friends for assistance. But they too were dumbfounded, and clearly hoping Jeff could avoid what was shaping up to become a nasty racial incident.

"Er…okay," ventured Jeff again, shakily. "Then I guess you could say you are a sort of mix of brown and…er…light grey."

"No, no!" screamed the policewoman, almost apoplectic with rage. "Look, you fool!" She held her two arms out in front of her body, palms open – "When I am this, I am red! And when I am this" – she waved her arms around wildly – "then I am green!"

41 Boiling Over

I began a new job with a Swedish aid project in Bulawayo. My task was to deploy teams of researchers into the townships at dusk. The mood in the Bulawayo townships was tense. My researchers, all Shonas, were dead scared to be working in "enemy" territory. Being the only white man on the darkened streets late at night, I also found the whole exercise extremely stressful. One night, after finishing my last run, I went down to the hotel bar for a well-earned drink. I entered the bar and scanned the room in search of anyone that might look like prospective company. It didn't look promising - some fat, suited government types, clearly drunk, jabbering loudly at one end of the bar, and an uncomfortable white couple, trying to look inconspicuous, in another corner.

I sat down at the bar and ordered a Castle. When the beer came, I sipped it in solitude. I considered my circumstances. It made depressing reading: my girlfriend had left me; my work was unrewarding; the country appeared to be headed for economic ruin; and young whites like me, with energy and talent to offer, were vilified as racist and were being deliberately sidelined from any meaningful role in the country's future. I slipped more and more into depression, silently bemoaning the lack of female company to distract me from my maudlin thoughts...

At first, I did not notice the drunken figure lurching out of the toilet. But as he staggered towards the bar, cheap suit awry, eyes glazed red, I realised he was headed in my direction. Silently, I willed him not to sit down. No such luck. The man crashed into the bar counter, then slumped onto the adjacent bar stool. His flabby bum crushed my foot which had been resting on the seat.

"Hey, *shamwari*" I said brusquely, "you're sitting on my foot."

There was no reaction.

"Hey, you! You're sitting on my foot!"

"Eh, wha-aati?" mumbled the drunk into his suit collar. Two bloodshot eyes struggled to focus on me.

"My foot. Get *off?*" I was spitting venom now. All my frustrations suddenly surged to the surface. The drunk swayed, but somehow remained seated. His beer-soaked breath oozed over me. "Ah, no.... Is not....," he slurred, then, incredibly, he turned and beckoned the barman to bring him another drink. Something snapped inside me.

"YOU STUPID SHIT!!"

The drunk turned to face me. "Ah, ah, don't call me that one, *marungu*. This is Zimbabwe now, not bloody Rhodesia."

I could take no more. I hit him.

It was only one punch, but the anger of everything that was tearing me apart went into it. I hit him because he was drunk and useless, like so many others. I hit him because of the smirking government officials at the end of the bar. I hit him because of the arrogance and hypocrisy of his one party state. And mostly, I think, I hit him because I felt I had lost everything: my girlfriend, my country, and all my hopes for the future.

The blow caught the drunk full in the chest, lifted him off the stool, carried him through the air and crashed him into a muffled, dribbling heap on the floor. I glared round the bar, waiting for someone to protest. One of the fat suited government men giggled. Then, as the barman reached for the phone, I spun on my heel, and marched out.

42 Of Lion and Elephant

I glanced around the near empty shelves of the hardware store. "I need a square-pin plug," I said to the bored-looking shop-keeper. We had stopped in Bulawayo for petrol and I had suddenly remembered I needed to change the plug on my electric shaver.

"Hard to get anything like that in this country," replied the shop-keeper. "All I can offer you is a second-hand one. It'll cost you fifteen dollars."

I did a quick mental calculation at the black market currency rate. "That's three US dollars, for a second-hand plug!" Avryl rolled her eyes in disbelief, clearly wondering why she had agreed to marry me and leave the comforts of a civilised life in South Africa.

I'd met Avryl while I was in self-imposed exile in South Africa, following the altercation with the drunk in the Bulawayo bar. I had been living in a communal house in Durban when a staggeringly beautiful blonde woman knocked on the door and announced she was responding to our advert for a room to let. As Avryl stood in front of me (I told my friends afterwards I thought she looked like Farah Fawcett-Majors), I could think of only two things: that I should definitely have cleared away last night's swathe of empty beer bottles, and that I had to do everything possible to make sure this gorgeous woman moved into our house.

I must have done something right, as she moved in shortly thereafter. Breaking all the unwritten rules of communal living, I then did my best to seduce our new housemate. I wined and dined her, pulled out my old jokes, and found myself enjoying life again for the first time in years. One evening, as we staggered back into the kitchen after a wild night on the town, I chanced my luck. "I just want to kiss you," I rasped in her ear in what I hoped was my sexiest voice. Happily, my wife-to-be didn't send me packing, and from then on our surreptitious love-affair blossomed under the noses of our housemates.

Now, newly married, here I was, back in Zimbabwe, introducing Avryl to the realities of a socialist command economy.

"It's up to you," the shop-keeper was repeating. "It still costs fifteen dollars. Like I said, you'll struggle to find anything in the shops these days." He was right about that. Shortages were rife in socialist Zimbabwe; not just of plugs, but everything: batteries; ballpoint pens; light bulbs; drinking glasses; bottles; matches; TV's; vehicle spares; toilet paper; and chocolate, to mention just a few. Buying a new car in Zim was an impossible pipe-dream. Even ordering a cool-drink at the local garage required a complicated process of swapping an empty Coke bottle first, before the attendant would let you drive away with a full bottle. Every car had a couple of empty cool-drink bottles rolling around on the floor in readiness for this national ritual. One could almost hear the collective "clunk" when city traffic turned a corner.

Zimbabwe had entered its second decade of independence still firmly in the grip of Mugabe's radical experiment with socialism. The early euphoria of independence had, however, long ago given way to a tangible national depression and sense of isolation. The rest of the world was progressing in leaps and bounds – the Berlin wall had fallen; the Cold War was over; apartheid had been swept away; and Nelson Mandela was now the darling of African politics. But Mugabe, isolated in his cocoon of self importance and pettiness, and surrounded by a retinue of praise-singers, presided over a country locked in a time-warp.

Over Avryl's protests, I bought the overpriced plug for my shaver and we continued on our journey. We drove towards Victoria Falls, the yellow swaying grasses along the roadside a mesmerising blur. Unlike in South Africa, there was almost no litter along the road – in a country of rampant shortages, the smallest plastic bag had value and a tin or a bottle was a prized possession. Throw away consumerism was unheard of here.

We met up with friends in Vic Falls, and took a three day kayaking safari down the Zambezi. "Now this is more like it," I said, as we glided past herds of elephant, and paddled down foaming rapids. The river trip came with all the extras - magnificent dinners served on white tablecloths; cold beer and toasted marshmallows around the camp fire; hot showers on the river bank. At night, the bush around us came alive with sound: hippos laughing like old men, nightjars purring, hyenas howling.

In our group was an aristocratic English lad. "What a wonderful evening," young Dicky enthused around the camp-fire, his wine glass sloshing dangerously in his waving hand. "In fact, it's *so* wonderful, I think we should toast the Queen." He stood up, raising his glass high. "To the Queen!" He glanced around expectantly. But Dicky had forgotten that he was supping with colonial rebels who, only a few years earlier, had fomented a full-scale revolt against the British crown. There was silence around the fire. After a suitably pregnant pause, someone found the words we were all looking for: "Dicky," Kevin muttered darkly, "if you can find me a stick long enough, I'd be more than happy to toast your fucking queen."

The next day, our guide paddled us along the edge of the river. We followed in our kayaks, Avryl and I in last place as usual (something to do with me not paddling hard enough, she said). A three metre bank rose sheer on our right hand side. Suddenly there was a terrific thundering and crashing on the riverbank. From our position at the end of the line of kayaks, we watched as two hippos, each the size of a wardrobe, launched themselves off the river bank into the safety of the water. The hippos just cleared the bow of the kayak ahead of us. Splooosh! Splooosh! Twin waterspouts erupted next to the kayak. Pete and Kevin, startled out of their reverie, held on grimly to the sides of their kayak as waves threatened to swamp them.

"Whoo hoo!" I shouted gleefully. "Hey guys, you're lucky hippos can fly, or you'd have them sitting in your lap!" Chuckling at their predicament, I didn't notice that our own boat was now being carried by the current right over the very spot where the hippos had sought deep water.

"Um... those bubbles, Graham?" pointed out Pete, now recovered from his near miss. "A bit less talk and a bit more speed might be a good idea about now."

"Shit, we'd better paddle!" Avryl and I bent frantically to our oars, whilst encouraging cries of "Just behind you!" from our fellow travellers lent wings to our efforts to clear the danger zone.

After our river trip, we joined another merry group of tourists on a four day walking safari at Kazuma Pan. Our guide, Leon Varley, started with a comprehensive safety briefing:

"If we are faced with a charging elephant, you MUST RUN," said Leon gravely. I duly made a mental note to self. Leon then covered buffalo, snakes, scorpions, poisonous plants, and unsafe water. Finally he got to the subject of lions. "If a lion charges, you MUST NOT RUN." I made another mental note.

The next morning we rose early to start our walk, but one of the German clients, emerging red-eyed from his tent, announced he was sick. "I am far too sick to go on this walk," he insisted. "I must return to my hotel." He did look a bit pasty, I thought, but hardly a hospital case.

"What sort of sickness is it?" I enquired confidentially as I helped him climb aboard a departing Land Rover.

"Oh, I'm not really sick," he confessed sheepishly, "I'm just terrified. All night I lay awake in my tent wondering what I must do if we come across a charging lion *and* a charging elephant *at the same time*?!"

43 Touching the Wild

"What will we see today?" The French tourist sitting behind me was clutching his video camera in one hand, his hat in the other, and was trying to keep his balance as we rocked and jarred along the bush track.

"Well, yesterday we saw leopard here," I shouted above the roar of the Land Rover engine, "so maybe we'll be lucky again. Keep an eye up in the trees."

That was the problem with FT's, foreign tourists - they had been brought up on a diet of National Geographic films and they assumed that Africa was wall to wall animals. The pressure was always on to find something, anything, to show them. The Hwange area, where we now were, had a lot of animals, for sure, but the thick bush and limited roads made it hard to find them or get close.

The bit about there being a leopard the day before was a lie, of course, but at least it would distract the tourists for a while. In the meantime, I had my work cut out trying to find where the hell I was! I knew where I had gone wrong. I had turned left, instead of right, at that last fork in the dirt track. But that was ages ago. Now I didn't recognise anything, and the thick thornbushes hemming us in on either side made it impossible to turn around. I had no choice but to follow this track to I knew not where....

Avryl and I had signed up as the new managers of the prestigious Sikumi Tree Lodge. Yesterday, Alan, my employer, had taken me on my familiarisation tour. We had stopped near a large bull elephant standing in the purple shade of an acacia. "These elephant belong to the Presidential Herd. They recognise our vehicles, so we can get really close," said Alan, edging the Land Rover closer. A wisp of blue diesel smoke stung my throat. Then Alan dug under his seat and dragged out a bag, from which he pulled a handful of acacia pods, tossing them on the ground. "They love these things," he said, "but just remember, only I should do this. The rest of the guides aren't allowed to feed the animals, okay?"

The elephant had been watching us with a rheumy eye. Now it came lumbering surprisingly quickly towards us, crossing the bare earth in giant quiet strides, until his immense grey, leathery bulk blocked out the sun. A red-brown watery eye gazed soulfully at me from less than a metre. Then, with a delicateness that belied its size, the beast swung its trunk across the ground, the tip gently flicking the dust, sniffing for the prized pods. One by one he found the grey, furry pods and popped them as delicately as chocolates into its deep pink mouth. He was close enough to touch. Finishing the last acacia pod, the elephant then moved to the front of our vehicle. It started to scratch its backside on the bull-bar. Our vehicle rocked wildly from side to side. Magnificent.

After a few minutes, the elephant turned and strolled back towards its shady tree, flicking trunkfuls of dust over his back as he went.

"You'll need to learn your way around here," said Alan, "so that if we are short of drivers, you can take some clients out on safari." That said, he then took me on a bewildering tour of one bush track after another. If I had realised I would be taking a full group of high-fee paying tourists out the very next day, I might have paid a little more attention to some of the landmarks along the way....

A loud scrunching sound underneath my vehicle brought me back to the present. I looked down to see what was making the noise, and saw that the surface of the dirt track that we had been following had changed to crushed granite chips. Not only that, but the road was now steadily rising ahead of us. As we slowly continued, the bush that had hemmed us in fell away on either side, and soon we could see over the tops of the surrounding scrub for kilometres around. "Ooh, aah!" marvelled the tourists as the vista revealed itself.

I wondered what the heck was going on as this strange granite chip road took a majestic wide sweep ahead of us. Then all of a sudden it dawned on me where we were. We had somehow gotten onto an old railway embankment!

I stopped the vehicle and looked around. The steep sides of the embankment dropped away either side into thick thornbush. There was no way down there. And there was no chance of reversing without risking tumbling off the edge. The tourists, eager for an explanation, beamed at me expectantly.

"Ahem," I coughed. "We might be able to see some elephant from up here." It was a poor bluff, but my clients swung their binoculars around enthusiastically.

While they were thus distracted, I noticed that further ahead the land appeared to rise up to meet our embankment. Perhaps we could get off there, I thought hopefully.

I crashed the Land Rover back into gear. "Keep looking for those elephant!" I shouted encouragingly to my passengers; we sailed boldly forward again along our embankment, like a ship on a canal, the churning gravel beneath us crashing like waves against our hull.

Finally I found an escape route and gingerly edged the vehicle down the side of the embankment. We reached terra firma – not a moment too soon, for I think some of the tourists would soon have smelt a rat - and suddenly, as if I had carefully engineered the whole sequence of events for my clients, there in front of us were thirty or forty elephant grazing gently amongst the trees, ignoring our din, and looking for all the world as if the noisy arrival of our vehicle was a daily event!

Living in the unspoilt bush among the animals was a childhood dream – and now I was living my dream. A rustic cottage, surrounded by teak forest, was our home. From the veranda we watched kudu and bushbuck grazing in the dappled shade on our lawn, and listened to the cacophony of the wild birds in the trees and the harsh bark of baboons. It was a patch of pure paradise.

When we left the cottage in the evenings to join the clients for dinner in the *boma,* we had to remember to switch on the single electric light bulb that illuminated the path between our cottage and the nearest guest house. If we forgot the switch, the return walk back to the cottage late at night, ears tuned to every rustle and creak in the pitch dark bush, always provided us with more adrenalin than we needed at the end of an evening!

One day, one of the tour guides fell sick. Avryl was summonsed at the last moment to take a group of elderly American tourists for a mid-morning game drive in a nice new Land Rover. "Just stick to the main road through the Park and you should be fine," I told her encouragingly, though thoughts of my earlier navigation debacle were still fresh in my own mind.

Things started off ominously when one old dear brained herself on the roll-bar as she climbed in to the vehicle. After a few consoling words, the safari set off. Squinting through the dust, Avryl gripped the wheel and clenched her teeth - the old codgers, mistakenly believing they were travelling with an experienced guide, chattered away, holding onto their hats, video cameras purring.

Their excitement was short-lived. Twenty minutes into the trip, after jolting along a particularly rough patch of road, Avryl felt a tap on her shoulder. She turned to find one of the clients throwing up all over the back seat. Stopping the car, she quickly ushered Mrs Vomit out of the vehicle, and held the old dear's forehead until she felt better.

Having done their best to clean up the mess in the car, the safari set off again. But more drama lurked around the next corner - a loud hissing sound from the rear announced a puncture. Avryl brought the vehicle to a halt. The sun beat down. Changing a wheel on a Land Rover in the dirt and heat was not in Avryl's book of fun things to do, so she conscripted all her male clients into the process of jacking up the vehicle, taking off the flat tyre, and replacing it with the spare. Then the safari recommenced.

A little while later, they came across a herd of elephants. Ah, things were looking up now, surely? Well, only if you ignore the fact that Mrs Vomit had started to feel queasy again. "Out of the car," snapped Avryl, not wanting to have to deal with another mess. Trying not to attract the elephants' attention, Mrs Vomit took up a position close by the front wheel, while the rest of the group cast worried looks at the nearby animals.

It had been a disastrous drive, the sun was blazing white overhead, hammering the bush into flatness, and no sane animal was venturing out into the heat. Avryl decided to call it quits. She loaded Mrs Vomit back into the car and turned towards camp.

Not so fast...A few metres down the track, the Land Rover coughed apologetically a few times and ran out of fuel. The fuel gauge breezily displayed "FULL".

"Don't worry, I'll get on the radio and call for help," Avryl reassured the worried clients. A good idea. That is, it would have been, if her radio was working.....

"OK, then we'll just *wait* here until someone comes along."

After what seemed like an eternity, another vehicle happened past. Everyone transferred into the second vehicle, the clients doubling up in each other's laps. The trip back to camp was, fortunately, without further incident. As the clients finally disembarked, one indomitable old dear was heard to remark "My word, Dorothy, now that's what I call a *real* safari."

"A couple of the tourists have come down with a stomach bug," said Avryl.

A twinge of trepidation. "Have any of the staff?"

"No."

"Then it must just be something they've picked up on the 'plane," I said, and dismissed the incident.

A few days later I was relaxing in a hot bath when a few short black hairs floated towards me in the bathwater. "Where did these come from?" I muttered. I glanced up at the thatched roof, which refused to answer. I topped up my bath with some more water, and realised the black hairs were coming, not from above, but from inside the water pipe.

"There must be a dead rat or something in the water tank," I said to Avryl. "I'll check it out tomorrow."

Early the next morning I strolled up to the water tank behind our house together with Steven, the foreman. The cool of night still lingered in the purple shadows under the trees, and green mosses grew slippery on the wet rocks around the tank. I jumped up on the edge of the tank and peered through the hatch down into the gloom. A dead bird floated on the surface. I fished it out with a stick, but there was nothing else unusual. . "Is there another water tank?" I asked Steven.

"Yes, boss. Over that side." He pointed into the forest across the *vlei.*

"Let's take a look then."

We walked the five hundred or so metres through the long yellow grass and into the forest. Once amongst the teak trees, we found a steel tower, some fifteen metres high, atop of which was a large rectangular water tank.

"Can't imagine anything could fall in there," I said to Steven, "but shoot up and take a look just in case."

Steven clanged up the metal ladder of the tank carrying a torch and disappeared on top of the tank. As I waited below, I gazed around, inhaling the early-morning sights. Africa was putting on its usual splendour – skittish impala approaching a nearby waterhole; yellow billed hornbills calling *"wukah wukah wukah"*; lappet-faced vultures circling on an early thermal.

There was a *"plop"* next to my feet. I looked down. Something brown had fallen next to me among the leaves. A dead bird perhaps? I leaned down for a closer look. Not a bird.... Suddenly I realised what I was looking at. A small hand. Five pink fingers and a dainty palm. A child's hand! Shocked, I poked at it with a stick..... No, not a child's.... there was dark hair all over the back of the small wrist.. I looked up. Steven was scampering his way back down the ladder.

"Is a dead baboon, baas!" he shouted excitedly. "But is all rotten and broking up!"

Grief, I thought, a baboon in the water tank! No wonder I'd got hairs in my bath.

Then suddenly I remembered about the clients getting sick. "Christ, Steven, we'd better turn off the water to the camp. *Checha!*"

We hushed it up, of course - brought in bowsers of clean water, made some excuse about the pump breaking down, and scrubbed out the tank with disinfectant. The strangest thing was, while the drowned baboon had been slowly putrefying week after week in the water tank, and the tourists had been dropping like flies, not one of the camp staff had fallen sick. Living in Africa had obviously given us some sort of immunity to the odd bug or two.

44 Renaissance

We had left Sikumi at the end of 1990, and were back in Harare. Avryl was complaining of persistent 'flu, so she paid a visit to the doctor who dramatically informed her that she was pregnant. The unexpected news that I was soon to become a father added urgency to my search for a new job. I found one in Durban. Weeks passed, then I received an urgent phone call. Over the long-distance hum and hiss that separated me from far off Harare, I heard my friend, Liz, twittering excitedly:

"Graham, your wife's gone into hospital. The baby's coming!"

"But it's not due for weeks!" I protested.

"Well 'dad', you'll just have to explain that to your baby. I'll call you when the blood sports are over."

I felt both irresponsible and helpless. "Look after Avryl," I said lamely, but the line was already dead. I booked a seat on the evening flight to Harare, and spent the rest of the day taking lessons from the ladies in the drafting office on how to fold a baby's nappy.

"I don't know whether it will be a boy or a girl," I protested to the clucking women.

"Then you'd better learn both nappies, hey."

Arriving back home, I was greeted by the sight of my new-born son contentedly asleep next to his exhausted mother.

"Twelve hours of labour pains, *then* they decide to do the caeser," Avryl grumpily informed me.

"Oh, shame," I said. I'd never had much of a bedside manner.

"And what did *you* get up to while I was going through all this pain?"

"Er, well, I had some beers at the airport," I admitted. "To celebrate, I suppose."

"Lucky you."

"Easiest birth I've not been at," I added cheerily. Avryl glowered. Some people, I thought to myself, just can't take a joke.

I fiddled with the car radio. On Radio One, the Finance Minister, Bernard Chidzero, was announcing the government's annual budget. I listened as we drove.

"Why do you want to listen to that?" asked Avryl.

"Ssh. Something funny's going on here," I hissed.

"Huh?"

"This speech. Chidzero is one of Mugabe's top people. Notice anything odd?"

"No. Sounds pretty boring."

"It is. Except for one thing which is really strange - normally these broadcasts go on and on with their political rhetoric. Always lots of references to the 'socialist struggle this' and the 'Marxist cause that' - even in the budget speech. Now, suddenly, nothing. In an hour of talking, this guy hasn't mentioned the word 'socialism' once. There's a sea-change happening here, I'm sure of it."

It turned out that I wasn't imagining things. Chidzero's economic reforms, when they were fully revealed, were nothing short of dramatic. Virtually overnight, the country shifted from dogmatic socialist economics to the free-market system: price controls were lifted, tax rates reduced, import and foreign currency restrictions eased, and overseas investors were encouraged to enter the stock exchange. Suddenly a new mood of optimism swept the country, and for the first time since

Mugabe took power, white Zimbabweans felt they once again had a meaningful role to play in the country's future. My business degree was now a sought-after commodity and I secured a management position in a retail company. The industry had for years been mired in a culture of inefficiency spawned by a lack of competition. Now, with the easing of business restrictions and a flood of imports and new players into the market, 'service' and 'efficiency' suddenly meant the difference between success and failure. Everything was up for grabs, everything could be changed. I felt an almost missionary zeal to drag my new company and its employees into the twenty-first century. I revamped every aspect of the business, and wielded a big hatchet, firing anyone who wasn't dynamic enough or who wouldn't embrace the new business ethic.

As Zimbabwe entered this new era, all around me – in business, sport, theatre, music - I sensed a new-found energy coursing through the nation's veins. White Zimbabweans, who for the past ten years had experienced only animosity and exclusion from their own government, now felt they were part of the nation again. Always proud of our African roots, but now fired by the country's new spirit of dynamism, we were now keen to embrace our fellow black Zimbabweans and integrate with the vibrancy of their indigenous culture. United at last, black and white Zimbabweans now determined collectively to show the world what our great little country could do.

The results of the country's renaissance were rapid and impressive: a new national cricket academy was launched, and the national cricket team, drawing on just 300 club players, began to hold its own against international Test teams. An international Arts Festival was launched to wide acclaim. Theatre and dance began to produce some quality talent. Local manufacturers began to innovate and export - Zimbabwean processed foods, beers, clothing and vegetables found their way onto shelves in supermarkets across the globe. Cut flowers were chilled and flown weekly to the world's largest auction house in Amsterdam.

As businesses, sport and entertainment began to flourish, more and more foreign visitors and investment poured into the country, the stock exchange boomed, and employment soared. It was, we all agreed enthusiastically, the very best of times.

45 A Quirky Place

After the debacle of me missing my son's birth, I felt some pressure to be present for my next child's entry into the world. So when Avryl announced her waters had broken, I was packed and ready. I had Avryl and her suitcase in the car in short order, and the three of us headed for The Avenues clinic. As my wife was wheeled towards the labour ward, I braced myself to witness my first live human birth.

"Sorry," said the surgeon, blocking my way, "this is going to be a caesarean. I'm afraid you'll have to wait outside."

"He'd better cut on the same scar," growled Avryl at me, as she was wheeled off into the operating theatre.

"Pity I didn't bring some beers," I proffered.

I paced the hospital corridors while the doctors took charge. Eventually a nurse re-emerged. "Mr Atkins? Congratulations. You have a daughter. She's in intensive care, but she should be fine. Would you like to see her?"

I did. I gowned up, and the nurse led me into a softly lit ward, where half a dozen tiny babies were asleep under glass domes, little aliens just arrived on spaceship earth. I glanced around. Where was my daughter? Then I spotted her – the only white baby in the room. I approached the incubator, and peered in. I couldn't believe how tiny she was. A feeding tube was inserted into her perfect miniature nose.

"She's beautiful," said the nurse.

"She is," I replied. To tell the truth, I was quite overcome.

Before we knew it, Kyle was at school-going age. After queuing all night, we managed to enrol him in Highlands government school, just over the road. One day, during his first term, it poured with rain. We hadn't gotten around to buying him a rain-coat, so in desperation we found a black plastic garbage bag, cut holes in the bottom and sides, and made him put it on. It would have to do. Then we delivered him to school. The sight of a skinny white boy sporting a dustbin bag to school must have been a sight to gladden the heart of any Marxist that happened to be watching.

At the end of the day when she collected Kyle from school, Avryl made a point of apologising to the headmistress for our son's unconventional garb.

"Oh, not to worry," replied the headmistress, "a couple of the black children also came like that today. Although," she added mischievously, "*they* managed to find *white* bags."

Both women looked at each other for a moment, then burst out laughing.

Life in a booming Third World environment was always going to be full of surprises, contrasts and quirky incidents, reflecting the nation's now rapid social and economic transition. Nowhere was this more obvious to me than with the new young workers in my stores. These guys, the product of the post-independence education push, were generally intelligent and delightfully willing and helpful. However, those from rural backgrounds lacked the sophistication of their urban peers. One day I overheard a shopper ask one of our new trainees if he could explain the difference between an Indesit washing machine and a Defy machine.

"Ah, yes madam," ventured the young man enthusiastically, "With this machine you turn the knobs, and with that other one you push the buttons."

"Er...okay then, can you tell me which is the better machine?" murmured the customer.

"Ah, certainly, madam. The Defy is a better machine. By far!"

"Oh, and why is that?"

"Ah, because my own mother, she has worked for many madams, and all of them have got a Defy."

Local TV, the last bastion of old-style socialist dogma, provided another window onto the melange of Zimbabwe's rapidly merging cultures, languages and technologies. Sometimes the offerings were almost bizarre - one day I happened to flick the channel onto a show called "It Takes Two". The aim of the show seemed to be to see if husband and wife would give similar answers to a series of questions. As I flicked on, the presenter was directing a question at the husband:

"Tell me, Langton," smirked the presenter, "which is the most unusual place that you and your wife have ever made love?"

"Oh, yes, that would be on a houseboat in Kariba," replied the husband, turning and beaming at the studio audience, which applauded enthusiastically.

The wife, who had been kept out of ear-shot in another room, was then called back into the studio.

"Agnes," crooned the presenter, flashing his pearly teeth at the nervous young woman, "Your husband has already given us the answer to this question. Now it is your turn to show us how well you know your man, and to give us the same answer. So, Agnes, please tell me, which is the most unusual place you and your husband have ever made love?"

Agnes' jaw fell open. "*Mai we,*" she gasped, mortified by the audacity of the question. "I cannot answer that!"

The presenter was unrelenting. "Please, Agnes," he insisted, "your husband has already given us this information. We now want your answer. I say again, Agnes, which was the most unusual place you have made love?"

The embarrassed woman was now hiding her face in her hands as the audience shouted encouragement. Agnes sneaked a peek at her husband. He beamed, gesturing encouragingly to assure her that everything was OK. Finally, her eyes glued to the floor, Agnes answered in a small voice, "The most unusual place was in my bottom."

One day a letter in the local Herald newspaper caught my eye. The writer of the letter, who signed himself "Fed Up", said he wished to alert the public to the outrageous customer service being visited on patients by the government health services. He demanded that the authorities do something about it. Apparently, Fed Up had gone to his local clinic in the suburbs to seek treatment for a "sexual infection". He had patiently joined a long queue, and presently a nurse appeared. The nurse proceeded to interrogate the patients one by one about their ailments.

"What is wrong with you?" the nurse demanded of one middle-aged man. The man replied with something unintelligible. "Speak up," the nurse demanded. The man gave another mumble.

"Oh! Syphilis!" boomed the nurse, "First door on the left!"

The queue of patients tittered amongst themselves, then shuffled forward. The next man in line was asked the same question. "VD," he mumbled.

"VD!" shouted the nurse. "Door on the left!"

Next in line was Fed Up. However, distressed by the display he had just witnessed, he decided not to go through the same public humiliation. When questioned as to the nature of his medical ailment, he whispered, "Headache".

"Headache! No problem. Two aspirin," boomed the bossy nurse, dispensing two pills. "Next!"

Fed Up now decided to seek more discreet service at a rural clinic. The wait in the queue this time was even more tedious, but eventually a nurse appeared. In a parade ground voice, the nurse addressed the assembled patients:

"Okay, all you ones with syphilis and VD, please form a queue here!"

Such quirky real-life incidents appealed to my tabloid-journalist sense of humour precisely because they were real. However, despite being steeped in decades of racial conditioning, I was careful to ensure that I only repeated such anecdotes, with their obvious racial undertones, when there were no blacks within earshot to take offence. I might have been a racist, but I still had manners and a sense of social propriety!

Despite the fact that blacks and whites now rubbed shoulders much more closely than before, especially in the workplace, social integration of the races, particularly the generations who had been through the war, was proving a slow process. The rantings of Mugabe and the state controlled media didn't help – theirs was a continuing daily diet of apportioning blame for every local problem on white conspirators either at home or overseas.

Even when I dismissed the government's propaganda as being simple paranoia, the psychology and culture of the "masses" - the rural populace - remained as mysterious and unfathomable as ever. My friend Lawrence told me how he was building a fine new house for his mother in a rural area.

"Graham, you won't believe the way our people at home think. My mother's new house has made her neighbours and friends so jealous. They are giving her such trouble now."

Lawrence's words sparked a memory of something my father had said, years earlier: "Never flaunt your wealth in Africa – it stirs up intense jealousy."

The social, economic and cultural divide between blacks and whites in Zimbabwe was slowly closing as an ever-greater proportion of the population shifted to the urban centres and came more closely in contact with the practices and values of an urbanised, westernised world.

But even Lawrence, a sophisticated, westernised African and as broad-minded a friend as any, still surprised me occasionally with his views. One day a group of us were walking together around a small farm which our boss used as his country retreat. It was natural and unspoilt, bursting with native vegetation and birdlife and a sanctuary for antelope that flitted through the bushes.

"Beautiful, isn't it?" I remarked. "Totally pristine. Wonderful."

"But he is not using this land for anything," objected Lawrence. "There are no maize fields or cattle. Nothing at all."

"It's not meant to be a working farm," I tried to explain. "It's a place where you come just to enjoy nature, to look at the view, listen to the birds."

Lawrence looked at me blankly. An agricultural tradition was obviously deeply inculcated in him, while my western aesthetic viewpoint was clearly an alien concept.

"There should still be some cattle," he grumbled. "Otherwise the land is wasted."

46 Michael

Mhaka Matare was born near Rushinga, in the Zambezi Valley, not far from where I was shot during the war. Growing up as a boy in the valley would have been as hard for him as for any rural kid in the country – water and firewood had to be collected, goats herded and protected from wild animals, a crop had to be somehow coaxed from the dry soils to feed the family, and malaria was endemic. When drought and war descended in the seventies, the tribes-people in the Zambezi valley found themselves caught up in the front-line of the conflict.

In his twenties, Mhaka left home to seek work and money in the city. He found a factory that was looking for a floor sweeper.

"What's your name?" the owner asked.

"Mhaka."

"OK, I'll give you a chance. You start tomorrow, Michael," said the owner. The anglicised version of his name stuck after that.

Despite his limited education and poor English, Michael was polite and hard-working. He also had a natural aptitude for fixing anything mechanical, and soon became a firm favourite with the boss. When the factory was forced to retrench a number of workers, the owner felt obliged to help Michael for his past loyalty and honesty, so he placed a job-wanted ad in the paper. We answered the ad, and the owner brought Michael to our house for an interview. "A better worker you'll not find," he assured us. Which is how Michael came to be our gardener.

Unlike many home owners who prefer manicured borders, bowling green lawns and whitewashed rocks along the drive, I have a penchant for allowing parts of my garden to go wild. I tried to explain my eco-friendly philosophy to Michael: "If it survives, it's good," I told him. "Any plant that just appears is a gift from God, so we allow it to stay." I have no doubt that Michael thought I was a little crazy.

I also have a real love affair with trees – I see them both as living sculptures and as shelters beneath which a cool micro-climate helps understorey plants to grow. I loved to plant rust-coloured *msasas*, thorny umbrella-topped acacias, *erythrinas* with their red coral flowers, and yellow barked fever trees. After much squinting from different angles, I would stick a pole in the ground and summon Michael. "I want to plant a tree here," I would announce. Michael rolled his eyes, knowing where this was leading.

"Sure?"

"Sure."

With much clanking and clattering, Michael would collect his pick, shovel and wheelbarrow and set to work digging the hole. At first, I would watch, but after a while, with the pick 'pinging' off the rocky ground, I felt it was better to leave the poor fellow to himself, and I would wander off to plan my next gardening project. If it was a weekday, I would put on the shoes Michael had already polished and drive into work in the car Michael had already washed that morning.

When I returned in the evening, a deep, square hole, emanating the rusty smell of newly turned red earth, would be awaiting my inspection. Often, unfortunately, after some more reflection (and not having had to endure blisters and back-ache myself), I would often confess to Michael, with some embarrassment, "Hmm, I don't think this is the best spot, after all. Tomorrow, I think you'll have to move the hole two metres that way." Michael never grumbled, and I always felt like a heel.

One night after we had held a dinner party, I banged on Michael's *kia* door around ten pm. "Michael, I need you to dig me a hole." Before he could conclude that I had gone completely bonkers, I explained that our labrador, Moby, had just died, and we needed to bury the body. Michael dutifully pulled on his trousers, collected his shovel, and selected a suitable spot to place the grave. Within an hour the task was complete. We woke the kids so that they could farewell their dog, then all retired again to bed.

Along with the precision siting of new trees, my other passion in the garden was having the perfect view, one of the reasons we had selected a new house in Borrowdale overlooking a small valley and a hillside of indigenous woodland. However, the best view was obstructed by a rock wall encircling the pool. "We'll have to get rid of this wall," I said. "What's the point of having a view if you can't see it?"

Michael was duly summoned, and tasked with knocking down sections of the wall. After several weeks work, again none of which raised a sweat on my own brow, Michael and I had created a series of delightful 'natural' windows overlooking the beautiful valley.

"Michael, you and I make a great team," I praised my weary gardener.

He smiled politely. "I think," he replied gravely, "next week, I go for leave."

47 A House of Cards

"Hey, want to hear a good joke?" said Marcus. We were huddled in a smokey corner of Sandro's nightclub.

I gave a quick glance over my shoulder, cautious of offending listening ears. "Sure."

"Okay, so two black caddies are walking on a South African golf course. They are following two white golfers down the fairway, and the one caddy says to the other caddy, 'Don't worry, brother, after the election, everything will be different. After the election, the masters will be the caddies.'

"Anyway, some months later, after the elections are over, the same four people are walking down the fairway. The white golfers are still in front, and the black caddies are still following with the golf bags.

"'Hey, Sipho,' says the second caddy, 'I thought you said everything would be different after the election?'

"'My brother,' Sipho replies, 'Do you remember I told you that after the election, the masters would be the caddies? Well, it is true. Now, *we are* the masters!'

"Ha ha ha," chuckled Marcus at his own joke.

But like many jokes, this one had a ring of truth. For, although the Zimbabwean economy was booming, and things seemed to be going well for the urban elite, life was not so rosy for millions of poor rural folk. Under the new free-market regime, free health and schooling had been scrapped, prices of staple foods had risen, and rural services had been cut back. As if this hadn't made life hard enough, a series of devastating droughts in the mid-nineties brought the peasants to the edge of starvation. Food relief, organised by government agencies, was sporadic and riven with corruption. As I travelled the country on business, visiting towns and far-flung rural centres, I saw haunting hunger stalking the land. Destitute families were flocking to the towns where they formed a new underclass – jobless, homeless and hopeless. Anger flickered in their eyes, especially the young who had been promised so much at independence. To make things worse, many whites, forgetting how powerful jealousy is in African culture, flaunted their newly acquired wealth. The poor, whose lives were now as fragile as wood-smoke, showed increasing hostility.

Some people say that Mugabe, seduced overseas by international acclaim and shielded by his praise-singers from bad news, simply overlooked the worsening plight of the rural poor in the country. Others say it was a situation that was to be expected, just another example of stereotypical Africa. Then again, others are more cynical - they point to the ease with which a dictator can manipulate a destitute peasantry. Keeping a peasantry wedded to a culture of handouts and party favouritism, they say, means that the ruling party is guaranteed of votes at election time.

Whatever the cause, by the mid-nineties the gap between rich and poor in Zimbabwe had never been wider. As the drought continued to bite, rural folk increasingly turned to stealing to make ends meet. Telephone wires, power cables, fences, and railway signalling equipment started to vanish. Cattle rustling, poaching, illegal gold panning and timber cutting, body-parts peddling, and car hijacking rates, all rose. To add insult to injury, the long-denied AIDS epidemic began to wreak havoc on traditional social structures. Within a few short years, the rural populace which had once been passive, kindly, honest and law-abiding, was now hungry, desperate, and primed for anarchy.

Other threads in the nation's fabric began to unravel too: inflation rose, driven by the government's reckless spending on luxuries and its unrestrained printing of money, and bribery and corruption began to flourish at all levels of government (Mugabe's ritual pardoning of politicians convicted of corruption and murder gave a green light for more of the same, and is perhaps the single biggest factor in Zimbabwe's ultimate demise). The rush to join the government gravy train soon had the many honest, hard-working blacks wondering why they should bother to keep to the straight and narrow when party patronage clearly was an easier route to success.

The stress of living in a society that now seemed to me to be more divided, corrupt and unsympathetic than ever before, began to tell on my frame of mind. I became increasingly short tempered. The growing number of beggars and "emergency taxis" on the streets, didn't help. I returned one afternoon to the office, scowling, my latest brush with a suicidal taxi driver fresh in my mind.

"Smile," said Vicky, my secretary, "Remember, you're the boss. Your employees expect you to smile all the time."

I scowled. "Zip it, Victoria. Let's just go for a drink. I think I need it."

I mentioned my growing fears for the country's future to a friend as we were returning from a business trip, our Air Zimbabwe flight on its final approach to Harare airport.

"I'm wondering whether I should consider emigrating," I said. "I'm not comfortable with this culture of bribery and exploitation."

"You're mad," my friend replied. "You can do anything in Zim. There are no rules! This is a place of opportunity! The country is just flying."

Suddenly our plane started to bank back and forth. The engine pitch changed, and we dropped sickeningly towards the ground. The nose of the plane rose, then dropped again. All the passengers went quiet, but there was no explanation forthcoming from the cockpit. As we finally made a scary, bumpy landing, I heard someone behind me comment, "Bloody hell, do you think the air hostess is flying this thing?"

Given the worsening plight of so many Zimbabweans, I thought it was a more appropriate question to ask of the country in general.

One day I found myself driving home behind a rural bus. Struggling up the hill, the bus spewed oily black smoke into my face. "Why should I have to breathe this shit?!" I cursed impotently. Then the bus drove straight past a three tonne weight restriction sign. "Just ignore every law!" I shouted. "Just drive wherever you fucking want!"

Suddenly something snapped inside me. I floored the accelerator and drove up alongside the bus, ignoring the oncoming traffic. Winding the passenger side window down, I hooted until the bus driver looked at me, then screamed at him, "Pull over! Stop your bus now!" The driver waved me away, which made me even more irate.

"The only thing standing between this country and bloody anarchy," I ranted to myself, "is law and order. If the bloody useless police won't enforce the law, I will!" I floored the accelerator again, pulled in front of the bus, then slammed on my brakes. Both our vehicles crabbed to a halt.

I leapt out the car and stormed towards the bus. "There's a three tonne limit on this road, sunshine!" I shouted at the driver, as he peered out his cab. The man looked more relieved that worried. Relieved I hadn't pulled a gun on him, no doubt. "Yes sir, I know," he replied politely.

"Then why the hell are you driving here?" I shouted. "I've got two kids who live along this road, and the road rules are there to protect them from getting run over by buses like this."

"I am very sorry, sir," replied the driver patiently. "I am taking the bus to park it at the boss's house." He pointed to show me his bus was in fact empty. Well, I must admit I hadn't noticed that before. And now I also became more aware of the face in front of me. No longer just another anonymous black face, but the face of a tired old man, wizened skin on his neck, deep lines furrowing his forehead, teeth yellowed from poor diet. His eyes had a worn-out look that told of an on-going struggle to feed and clothe his own family while life got harder and harder around him. What challenges and tribulations had this man witnessed, I suddenly wondered, about which I knew absolutely nothing?

My jumbled thoughts submerged my earlier anger. "I'm sorry," I muttered guiltily. "It's just......" But I couldn't explain why I had needed to vent my submerged rage on him. This man was, I now realised, as much a victim in this mad country as I. I waved him away.

As the bus manoeuvred back into the traffic, I sat down, trying to control the despair I felt welling up in my chest. I cursed; this is *my* road, *my* city, *my* park, *my* country....

With sudden clarity, I realised that here was the core of my problem: I had huge emotional ownership in this country. Zimbabwe was the land of my birth, my children were fourth generation. We – my family and my tribe - had painstakingly built this nation and its infrastructure over generations. Like middle-class missionaries most of us had also tried to spread a gospel of honesty, fairness and integrity. Now, emasculated by Mugabe's new elite, we were being forced to watch as the entire fabric of our country – roads and railways, hospitals and schools, sports clubs and libraries, forests and game reserves, freedom of the press, the rule of law, professionalism, respect for the judicial system - were systematically and deliberately trashed. The potholes in the road were not just potholes to me, the eyes of a beggar not just another hungry face; instead these things spoke of a deliberate, orchestrated destruction of *my* country, its future and its people.

"This place is like a house of cards," I said to Avryl when I got home. I told her about my run-in with the bus driver, and the flood of thoughts the incident had prompted. Then I described to her the scenes of poverty and desperation that I had begun to notice in the rural areas. I found my worries pouring out in a torrent of complaint and trepidation.

"The problem with Mugabe is that he feels an obligation to look after his immediate family, and also his extended clan, but he feels no obligation to look after anyone else in this country." I kicked a chair in frustration. How the man could ever claim to be a socialist was beyond me.

"You know," I concluded, "one day, it's all going to blow. And when it does, *everything* will come down."

Avryl listened in silence, not interrupting. After I finished, she looked at me thoughtfully. "I agree with you," she said, "and it's the kids' future we need to think about. What happens if we have to get them out? All they have are Zim passports. Where will they go, and how will we educate them?"

"I don't know," I replied miserably. We eyed each other silently. Once again I realised my own world was facing ruin, my optimistic dreams for the future lost once more. Then, hoping to catch my last shred of optimism before it danced mockingly out the window, I took a deep breath. "I guess we must start looking at some new options. We can still make good money here. We'll just have to move as much cash off-shore as possible. In the meantime, you, dear wife, can work out where the hell we should go."

"Right," she replied, "let's do it. And let's just hope the wheels don't come off this country before we're ready to leave."

Above: Cocking a snoot at Mugabe. Colonial party, Harare, Nov 1981.
Below: Avryl and I, Cape Town, 1989

Top: Elephants at Kanondo waterhole
Above: Our bush cottage at Sikumi, Hwange
Right: Minefield remaining after the war
Below: Kayaking on the Zambezi River

Avryl with Kyle
(right) and Chelsea
(below right)

Kyle with Sam
(below)

Kyle and
Chelsea

Our pool and garden, with msasa trees and aloes, at 27 Rayden Drive

Above: As Managing Director of Tedco Retail, with Branch Managers, 1995

Below: First Street, Harare, 1999, and one of the Innscor stores that I managed

Left: Reinforcing the back door prior to the 2000 elections. Violence, farm invasions and intimidation were rife across the country

Below: Michael (Mhaka) hard at work

48 *Jambanja!*

In 1997, a small group of protesters marched up Borrowdale Road and assembled outside Mugabe's official residence. As the presidential guards eyed the crowd and cocked their AK 47's, the protesters chanted slogans, waved placards, and sang revolutionary songs.

It was not unusual to see sporadic anti-government demonstrations in Harare. I had often driven past the university when it was closed by student protests. Price increases in staple commodities like bread invariably sparked riots, and more than once our company employees had been trapped in our city offices by clouds of teargas drifting through the streets of the capital. But public displays of discontent were always quickly and ruthlessly crushed by the riot squad that was always on stand-by. (It was a standing joke that it was quicker to get a response from the police by reporting a riot than by reporting a murder.)

But strangely, that small protest in 1997, which normally would have been brushed away by the baton-wielding riot squad within minutes, prompted no official retaliation. It soon became clear why; the protesters were war veterans, demobilised foot-soldiers from Mugabe's original guerrilla army. The veterans' slogan during the liberation struggle had been "One settler, one bullet". But nearly two decades after the war was over, the white settlers, their original enemy, were prospering on farms and in business, while most war veterans, poorly educated, remained destitute and hungry. Lacking even a war pension and at their wits end, a few of the veterans had decided to appeal for help from the one man they still believed had their interests at heart, the patron of their association, Robert Mugabe himself.

Mugabe could deal with criticism from any enemy. But protest by his loyal foot-soldiers was like a slap in the face. He realised then that he had ignored for nearly two decades the very people he proclaimed as heroes. Possibly he even felt some guilt. So instead of crushing the veterans' protest, Mugabe made a rash public promise to them; a raft of financial benefits were to be granted to every war veteran: $50,000 as a lump sum payment, $2,000 a month pension for life, as well as various other perks.

Within days of Mugabe's announcement, tens of thousands of people, many too young ever to have seen action in the war, were mobbing social welfare offices country-wide, all claiming to be war veterans and demanding a share of the loot. This, they realised, was a chance not only to get on the gravy train, but to partake in an orgy of largesse authorised by the highest voice in the land.

Foreign investors looked on aghast. You didn't have to be a financial genius to do the sums; the Zimbabwe government would be broke within months. The investors made the only reasonable call they could – get every dollar out of the country as fast as possible. Foreign funds began to pour out. The stock-market immediately crashed, and the Zim dollar halved its value overnight. The financial bloodbath became known as Black Friday. It was the day the keystone was removed from the house of cards.

To help pay for the new war vet pensions, the government increased sales tax and excise duty on fuel. The price of maize meal, the staple food, was hiked by 36%. Cooking oil rose 60%. Average black families who were already struggling to make ends meet now found it almost impossible to survive.

To protest the worsening economic conditions (the cost of basic food had now risen 500% since Mugabe took power), the trade union movement called a three day general strike. On the first day of the strike, riot police fired tear gas at a small group of demonstrators in Harare city. More people joined the protest, and before long the police lost control of the situation. Full scale rioting now erupted, leaving the city centre looking like a war zone.

After a second day of riots, many people began to believe that perhaps the government was on the back foot; that for the first time since independence people-power was now the force that was shaping events in the nation.

They couldn't have been more mistaken. That night, the army was deployed into the townships. Running from house to house, soldiers dragged people from their houses into the streets, beating men, women and children mercilessly.

This hard ball response from the government snuffed the energy out of the protests for the moment. However, over the next two years worsening economic conditions continued to fuel rising dissatisfaction with Mugabe's government. The President's decision in 1998 to send troops to the Democratic Republic of Congo to shore up the government there added to the country's economic woes. Inflation reached 50%, and fuel shortages became widespread

In 2000, Mugabe asked his citizens to vote in a referendum on proposed changes to the constitution that would extend his term as President. Up until then, Mugabe had never had to worry about opposition to his wishes. In the forefront of the revolution that had wiped away white rule, he had swept every election since. But by 2000, things had gotten tough for the average Zimbabwean, and now an opposition voice had arisen – the Movement for Democratic Change. The MDC, headed by veteran trade-unionist Morgan Tsvangirai, accused the ruling ZANU-PF party of being responsible for the economic meltdown in the country and of ignoring the worsening plight of ordinary people. To make their dissatisfaction known, the MDC urged voters to defy Mugabe at the referendum.

Referendum day came and I gave our gardener, Michael, a lift to the nearest voting booth. As we drove, I quizzed Michael. "Do you know what this referendum is about, Michael?"

"I know," he replied with quiet confidence.

We turned into the parking area near the voting booth, and parked under the shade of a large jacaranda tree. A few steps away, we joined a small queue which was inching its way towards the doorway of a sagging khaki tent. At this time of the morning it was mostly domestic workers in the queue. The atmosphere was restrained, but purposeful. Three armed policemen stood nearby, chatting and joking amongst themselves, ignoring the voters. The queue shuffled forward, and I found myself inside the tent in front of a battered wooden desk.

"ID?" asked the official behind the desk. I produced my aluminium ID card, and he glanced at the photo.

"Hands," he demanded. He inspected my fingers under an ultra-violet lamp, looking for signs of the fluorescent ink that would indicate if I had already voted. Satisfied, he gave me a voting paper and directed me to a shaky wooden booth.

I studied the ballot paper. Not hard to do, this, just a cross next to 'Yes' or 'No'. Another official stood disconcertingly close. I tried to ignore him. I picked up a pen tied to a piece of dirty string, wondering if realistically there was any point at all in my bothering with this voting business. Then, resolved to do my duty, I put a bold cross on the 'No' box. Behind me, the official shuffled his feet. And that was it. I waited for Michael to finish casting his vote, then we headed our separate ways, he to tame the ever encroaching jungle in our garden, I to sell more TV's to people who could no longer afford them. Neither of us spoke about what was really on our minds.

No-one was more surprised than President Mugabe when the referendum votes were counted. For the first time since independence, the nation had defied the president's wishes. Appearing on TV, 'Uncle Bob' announced the results in a stony, clipped monotone. There was none of his trademark fist waving and pompous speech-making. His lips were thin and pursed with tightly contained emotion, as he confirmed that the referendum had delivered an overwhelming 'No' vote.

"Jesus," I said, "he'll be really pissed off about this."

Up until then, Mugabe had tolerated the presence of whites in Zimbabwe because they had largely remained uninvolved in politics. But now, convinced that his referendum defeat had only happened because white farmers had encouraged their farm labourers to vote against him, Mugabe decided that the unspoken ethnic pact was now over. He determined to crush the white farmers and destroy their influence. Within days of the referendum, we got a taste of how he intended to achieve this. A rag-tag army of war vets and unemployed youths was unleashed onto scores of commercial farms around the country. The invaders, chanting and beating drums, besieged farmers in their houses. They intimidated and tortured farm labourers, killed cattle, horses and dogs, set fire to fields, cut down trees, erected roadblocks to prevent rescue parties, and began to peg stands for themselves. When terrified farmers phoned the police for help, they were told it was a 'political matter', that the police had been instructed not to interfere. By the middle of March, 500 farms were 'occupied'.

The first white farmer to die was a prominent MDC supporter, David Stevens. Stevens was abducted by armed men and murdered on 15th April. On the 18th April another farmer, Martin Olds, also an MDC supporter, faced a hit squad of a hundred men brandishing AK-47 automatic rifles who arrived at his farmhouse in a fourteen vehicle convoy. After a three hour gun battle with his assailants, Olds ran out of ammunition. Injured, and barely able to move, he crawled out the door and surrendered. He was beaten to death by the mob. The police made no arrests.

Across the country, the situation was the same. Flying back into Harare from a business trip, everywhere I looked the air was thick with brown smoke and I could see unchecked fires raging across Mashonaland's commercial farms. *Jambanja*, the war vets called it, turning everything upside down.

Although the invasions were clearly co-ordinated and well financed, the government insisted they were not behind it, that *jambanja* was a "spontaneous" reaction by a land-starved people. They refused to explain why government buses and trucks were collecting unemployed youths from the streets and carrying them to white farms with promises of free land and a $50 daily payment. Nor was there any reassurance that the government might act to stop the illegal occupations. "You don't solve a problem by cracking down on the effect," a government spokesman sneered. On the contrary, the government soon began listing farms for compulsory acquisition. With war vets snapping at their heels, more and more commercial farmers were driven off their properties. By mid May, over 1400 of the 5000 commercial farms had been occupied, twenty people had been killed, and a thousand cases of torture had been recorded by human rights groups.

Redressing the "historical imbalance" in land ownership now became the focus of the government's campaign for the forthcoming elections. Full-page adverts appeared in the press urging the people to support ZANU-PF, with the catch-cries "Land for the People" and "We will never be a colony again".

The opposition MDC pointed out that Zimbabwe had been independent for two decades and that the economic mess was due to corruption and mismanagement under Mugabe's rule. Mugabe shot back that the MDC were simply British lap-dogs and puppets. Lost in all the tumult were the inconvenient truths about land ownership:

1. Whereas at independence roughly half the agricultural land was owned by whites, twenty years later 40% of white-owned farmland had, with the assistance of funding from Britain, been bought by the government. However, much of this land had simply been given to the new political elite, Mugabe's cronies, rather than to the poor.

2. By 2000, 8 out of 10 white farmers were farming on land which the government had already declined to purchase under its own right-of-first-refusal laws.

3. Although the country was at peace, the government preferred to spend many times

more dollars on the military than it allocated to land acquisition

As the elections drew closer, Mugabe dropped all pretence of racial tolerance and began venting his long-held racial prejudices in public. "The white man," he announced at an election rally, "is not indigenous to Africa. Africa is for Africans. Our party must continue to strike fear in the heart of the white man, our real enemy, they must tremble!"

On the other side of the globe, western nations, aghast at the meltdown of a country they had uncritically hailed as a model of democracy, found themselves caught out by the sudden turn of events. Worse, having turned a blind eye for so long to Mugabe's persecution of black people, they now found themselves unable to protest too strongly about the plight of white farmers lest they be accused of playing racial favourites.

49 The Storm

"Mr Atkins?"

I glanced up from my newspaper. A well groomed woman was standing in front of me. "We can take you down to your safety deposit box now." She displayed a bunch of keys in her hand. Her fingernails were immaculately manicured, and she had an expensive gold bracelet around her narrow wrist.

"Thank-you," I replied.

We were joined by another bank employee, and the three of us entered a small lift. One of the women turned a key, and the lift descended silently. The two employees, clearly happy to be away from their desks, struck up an animated conversation. As they switched back and forth between English and Shona, I picked up snatches of their chatter - something to do with a boyfriend being unfaithful. Ironic, I thought, how everyone keeps behaving normally while out there, beyond the comfortingly thick walls of Barclays Bank, life as we know it is falling apart. Fields are burning, people are being murdered, and farms which have taken generations to build are being ruined overnight...

"Here you are, Mr Atkins."

I jolted back to reality. We were in the basement, and the heavy gates of the vault were swinging open. "Just use your key there." She pointed, indicating a small metal drawer with a number on the outside. "Let us know when you are finished." She turned, and joined her companion in the lobby, leaving me to open my safety deposit box in private.

I unlocked the metal drawer, and withdrew a small tin box. It was heavy for its size. That didn't surprise me, considering the contents. There was a small table in the middle of the vault. I placed the tin box on it, and opened the lid. The glint of gold greeted me. There was a selection of jewellery, plus some precious stones in small bags, and a small wad of US dollar bills. I tipped the jewellery onto the table – it made a musical tinkle. But I had not come for that. My hand delved deeper into the box, and slowly I withdrew another, smaller box. This one was only made of cardboard, indeed it was scuffed and tattered, and clearly had once housed golf balls. But now it hid a more menacing bounty. I opened the lid, and unwrapped the yellow cloth inside. The shiny steel of my father's 9mm pistol gleamed at me. This was what I had come for.

I picked up the pistol gingerly. It felt surprisingly heavy in my hand, but the balance was familiar. Echoes of a long ago war. I put the pistol back in its cardboard box, glancing in the direction of the door as I did so. The two women were still out of sight, engrossed in conversation. I pulled a plastic shopping bag from my pocket. It had a "Truworths" logo splashed across it. Quickly now, I hid the box in the bottom of the Truworths bag. Next I found the ammunition. I remembered what had happened to Martin Olds when he ran out of ammunition, and decided I might as well take it all. I wrapped the ammo in newspaper, and placed these smaller bundles in the Truworths bag also. Then I took off the jersey I had been wearing, and placed it inside the bag, concealing its contents.

I had what I needed. Quickly I put the jewellery back and locked the safety deposit box away again. I checked myself over – there was nothing obviously out of place, I looked like someone carrying a shopping bag of clothes. Hopefully it wouldn't attract any attention. I stepped out of the vault.

"All done, thanks," I said to the two ladies.

I waited while they secured the vault. A few moments later, and I was whisked back to the main foyer of the bank. "'Bye!" the two ladies chimed in unison.

I headed for the front door. This would be the most dangerous spot. More than one person carrying a bag out of the bank had been mugged in recent months. I stepped out into the street, the bright sun momentarily blinding me. I glanced across the road. The lunch-time crowd was thinning. *If anyone is watching me, will I be able to spot them?* I turned left, up the pedestrian mall, walking casually but briskly. The urge to turn around was overwhelming. Instead I looked at reflections in the shop windows. No-one seemed to be following me.

I reached the safety of the car park where I had left my Land Cruiser.

"Morning, Robson."

"Morning, sah," replied the guard. With the prevalence of car theft, every car park had a security guard. It was just one of those things we had all gotten used to.

I opened the rear door of my Land Cruiser. I had already planned where to hide the bag – in a small tool compartment in a side panel. I slipped the bag into the compartment, then shut it with a *click*.

"Sir?"

I jumped. The security guard was standing right behind me.

"Yes, Robson?" I could feel my throat tighten. I was sweating.

"Sir, you haven't forgotten that job for my brother?"

I let out an audible sigh of relief. "No, Robson, I haven't forgotten. I'll let you know if we have a vacancy." Everyone was desperate for work. "I must go now," I said brusquely.

I climbed into the Cruiser and reversed out the parking bay. As I drove out the gate, the security guard saluted.

I headed home. Carrying an unauthorised firearm was risky, but it was a risk I had to take. Tension in the country had reached fever pitch. For the first time in twenty years of living in Zimbabwe, I was really scared. If my family was attacked in our house, we knew the police would ignore any plea for help. The pistol, and a pre-planned escape route down to the bottom of the garden, were all my family would have to rely on if it came to the worst.

I decided it was best to avoid driving past Mugabe's official residence, so instead of taking my usual route along Borrowdale Road, I took a longer route along Second Street. But as I turned past the university, the worst possible thing happened: a row of whitewashed 44-gallon drums blocked the street - a police roadblock.

"Fuck it!"

There was no avoiding the roadblock. To turn around risked bringing on a hail of gunfire. A policeman wearing a reflective vest flagged me to a stop.

"Where are you going?"

"Home," I replied cheerily. "Working half day today." The policeman looked sideways at me. "So I can have a good party tonight," I added.

Suddenly the cop grinned - there seemed to be nothing more important to these Shona than a good party.

"Maybe you have some beers for your party, huh?" he fished, casting an eye around the back seat of the car.

"Yes, plenty, my *mukka*, but I've already taken them home."

The cop laughed. "OK, then, you can go."

"Thanks."

As I eased the car away from the roadblock, I heard a banging in my ears. I realised it was the sound of my heart beating wildly.

I drove out on Borrowdale Road, towards home. My mind was in turmoil – after my own war experiences, I had foresworn guns and violence as a solution to any problem, yet here I was, having to break that promise in order to protect my family against thugs and murderers while the police stood idly by. Why had the world let this happen to our young country? Why hadn't civilised nations spoken out against Mugabe earlier on? Why did South Africa, fresh from its own struggle against the evils of apartheid, now refused to condemn Mugabe's rule of terror? I thumped the steering wheel in frustration. I just wished the bloody Australian embassy would speed up our immigration request. A man could die out here, waiting for the wheels of bureaucracy to turn in Canberra.

I passed a row of election posters taped to street lights which no longer worked. The face of ZANU-PF's candidate for Harare East sneered down at me. VOTE FOR COMRADE STALIN MAU-MAU! - a blatant resurrection of old *chimurenga* names and war hostilities that were supposed to have been buried two decades ago.

"Bloody bastard," I cursed. I vowed I'd be there on election day to vote against Robert Mugabe and Mr Mau-Mau, no matter what.

I called Avryl on my mobile. "Hi. I'll be home in five minutes. Can you unlock the gate." With crime soaring

out of control, a phone call home was a standard precaution
– to stop at your gate was risky in these days of rampant car
hijackings. I instinctively glanced in my rear view mirror.
Was that blue car following me? Again, not paranoia, just
prudent behaviour in these dangerous times. The traffic
light ahead turned red. Damn it! I slowed down, willing
the light to change to green. The blue car was right behind
me now, and a slow panic crept through me. I decided not
to take any chances and gunned the engine, shooting
straight through the red light. The blue car didn't follow, so
I could relax again.

As I drove, the sun was setting in a ball of red to my
left, singeing the bottom of clouds with scarlet, and
splashing a stately row of gum trees with crimson and gold.
Cows grazed in the fields. In the distance a horse trotted,
pepper puffs of dust rising up from its hooves. I loved this
semi-rural scene out here on the edge of the city. I
recognised a hand-written sign on the side of the road
advertising fresh chickens for sale. Each day as I
approached this sign, I tried to guess beforehand what the
new price of chickens would be - the prices seemed to
double each week.

I slowed and turned off the main road into Rayden
Drive. Nearly home now. There would be a cold beer
waiting for me, and the kids would probably mob me and
plead with me to go for a swim with them…

Suddenly, in front of me, the normally quiet street
was clogged with people. It was too late to turn around, so I
braked, quickly winding up my window as I did so, and
checking the doors were locked. The throng blocked the
whole road, there were ragged women and dusty children
everywhere. I noticed a few older youths waving canisters.
Tearful, angry faces peered through the windscreen,

shouting at me. What were they saying? What did they want?

"Manzi, manzi." Water, water. Then I remembered - the municipal water supply had failed four days earlier. These people must be from the nearby Hatcliffe township – desperate and thirsty, they were now roaming the neighbouring richer suburbs, searching for that most basic commodity.

Realising I was not immediately a target, I eased the car gently forward and the crowd, sullen, parted and let me through. Once I was past, I accelerated quickly. It was only fifty metres to our driveway. I saw Avryl standing at the gate, peering down the road. Our two dogs, Sam and Cindy, were standing either side of her, hackles raised.

"Quickly, lock the gates," I shouted as I drove in. "If they find out we have a swimming pool we'll have a riot on our hands!"

I drove down the drive, msasa pods crackling beneath the tyres, and parked near the house. Fortunately, neither our house nor the swimming pool was visible from the street. I looked back, relieved to see Avryl walking back down the driveway. At the gate the dogs were now barking and snarling, putting on a great show of viciousness. The sullen crowd passed by on the far side.

I gave my wife a hug. "So, how's your day been?"

"Oh, you mean apart from having to get water from the swimming pool and having no electricity? Well, I couldn't get any bread at the shops, and I've spent the last three hours in a petrol queue. So, other than that, it's been bloody wonderful."

"Sorry." I wished I hadn't asked.

"If I hear one more person tell me the lifestyle here is still great, I'm going to hit them."

"Sorry." Again.

"I changed some more money on the black-market, today. Eighty to the US dollar, can you believe? Shit, Graham, do you know how nerve-wracking it is walking out the bank with a gym bag full of cash under your arm?"

"I'm sure. Just make sure you get straight into your car when you're carrying that much money."

"It's not that easy. As soon as you're out the bank, the bloody vendors are all over you. Some bugger stood right in front of me trying to sell me roses today, and while he was standing there, he dripped water all over my new suede shoes. Christ, I was so cross."

I changed the subject. "Let's grab a beer and take a walk down to the river." We called Sam and Cindy and the dogs appeared wagging their tails, knowing this was their walk time.

We stepped down from the veranda and strolled across the lawn, past the swimming pool. The scent of jasmine and ripe mangoes mingled in the air and purple crested louries called in the branches of the trees. The dogs raced in front and disappeared down the hill in search of rats and lizards. We followed slowly, savouring the cool breeze that was blowing up the valley. Amidst the veld grasses, thousands of *cosmos* flowers, white, pink and crimson, waved a cheerful greeting in a beam of evening sunlight.

We walked to the end of the garden until we could see the river at the bottom of the garden. In the long grass below us, we could see Sam and Cindy pouncing from tuft to tuft, trying to flush out small prey. Weaver birds swizzled and chirped in the reeds, and a gymnogene eagle swooped overhead, searching for a meal of new-born chicks. We sat down on a bench under an old *msasa* tree and soaked up the beauty of this small patch of paradise. In the distance a thunderstorm grumbled over brooding distant blue-grey hills.

We sat in silence for a long time. The distant thunderstorm grew closer and bigger, massive cumulonimbus clouds billowing thousands of feet into the sky, pushed up on the last of the day's heat. Soon the clouds had blotted out the sun, and the warmth of the day was extinguished. The wind picked up, bringing a smell of rain on dry earth, and carrying snatches of tinny African music from someone's far away radio. Around us yellow leaves whisked in the stiffening breeze, splattering the gathering evening gloom with whirling patches of gold. Overhead the skies grew dark and angry. Thunder rumbled closer, the sound of gods moving their furniture. The dogs had come back to us now, nervous with the approach of the storm. They sat close by our legs, warm and skittish. A goshawk flashed across the valley, fleeing the storm.

"This really *is* Africa," I mused aloud. "These sounds, the smells, this beauty all around us. It's beyond words." I sighed. "On the one hand we have this, and on the other…" - I jerked my head over my shoulder – "we have to put up with all that crap back there." I took a swig of beer. "They always say the last thing to run out will be the beer - thank God."

"You work with lots of decent, sensible blacks," said Avryl. "Can't they change the way things are going?"

"I'm sure they'd love to," I replied, "but together with the whites, those are the very people Mugabe is intent on forcing out of this country. He's doing what Stalin did. Get rid of the educated middle classes, then control the peasants through brute force."

"You know," I continued, "it always comes from the top. If you have a person at the top who says corruption, nepotism, theft will be rooted out and punished, it sets the tone for behaviour all the way down the line. But if you have a President who openly incites hatred, racism, violence, then he gives a green light to thuggery and favouritism right across the country. It was the same with Stalin. He set the tone for fear and persecution for thirty years. Things only began to change when he died."

Avryl and I looked at each other glumly. These were thoughts that we had preferred to keep buried over the last few years, rather than having to face up to a growing realisation that Zimbabwe was finally going the same way as the rest of black Africa. The worst racists had always predicted this, and we had always hoped they would be wrong.

We sat and watched the storm rolling towards us up the valley. "At least if it rains those people will get some water," said Avryl. "And if we ever get to Australia," she added, "I won't miss the bloody petrol queues, that's for sure."

"Some people say that after living in Africa, Australia is boring."

"Right now," Avryl replied, "boring sounds just fine."

The lightning slashed and danced closer and closer. Rolls of thunder tumbled angrily through the tops of the trees. Heavy, pregnant drops of rain began to fall, slapping the branches above us and slamming into the dry ground, flinging up specks of red soil. A blinding crack of lightning smacked into the hillside opposite. The dogs bolted for the house.

The rain was racing towards us in a solid sheet, just metres away. I thought I should feel vulnerable and exposed with the lightning, the howling wind and the gathering force of nature unleashing itself around me, yet instead I felt a strange sense of immunity, a remoteness, as though I could just stand there and watch as it hurled its wrath at the trees and grass and dirt, and I would be left untouched.

"We'd better go back,' said Avryl.

"I suppose."

Another bolt of lighting sizzled overhead and the thunderclap took my breath away.

"Come on, run!" urged Avryl. "We'll just make it if we hurry. We can always come back again when it's all over."

50 June 2000

The elections were held at the end of June. After months of violence, an eerie calm seemed to descend on the country, and on election day, I, with millions of my countrymen, headed to the polls. The number of polling booths in the city had been drastically reduced by the authorities in an effort to frustrate urban voters from casting votes for the opposition, and when I arrived at the polling station, the queue was already several hundred people long. Undeterred, blacks and whites stood in line in jovial mood, determined to do their bit for the country's future.

Unless they were employed by the military or government, tens of thousands of citizens outside the country were not allowed to vote. Thousands of farm workers who had had their ID's destroyed or stolen during the farm invasions were unable to vote. Thousands of people whose names had mysteriously vanished from the voters register were unable to vote. And after months of intimidation and violence, scores of dead and seriously injured simply did not make it to the polls.

With 2,5 million votes cast, ZANU-PF polled a mere 34,000 votes more than the opposition MDC, giving Mugabe's party a narrow 4-seat majority. But, with a constitutional amendment that conveniently allowed the President to appoint a further thirty unelected persons to parliament, Mugabe retained an unassailable parliamentary majority.

Against a backdrop of suspicion and allegations of rigging, the EU's election observer noted, "The term 'free and fair elections' is not applicable in these elections."

Predictably, the South Africa observer mission disagreed, and gave the results the all clear.

With the election over and democracy once again thwarted, there was, I now knew with certainty, absolutely no hope left for Zimbabwe. I sensed a little of what it must have been like to be a Jew in Nazi Germany during Hitler's rise to power - the feeling of time running out, of doors closing, the stench of moral decay assailing one's nose, and all around the drumbeat of evil on the march.

It was time to get the hell out.

51 Farewell

The Australian visa stamps were finally in our passports. Our furniture had left in a shipping container. Friends had offered to put us up for our last night in Harare.

Avryl and the children had left the house first, their car bouncing down the red dirt driveway for the last time. As they turned out the gate, a sigh drifted though the dark green leaves of the *msasa* trees, and a crested barbet purred sympathetically overhead. The double iron gates at the end of the driveway drooped despondently - there was nothing more for them to protect. A wet muzzle sniffed my hand, as Sam sought my attention. I patted his brindled head. Cindy trotted up for a pat too. Both dogs sensed my mood, and slunk close to my side. I listened to the barbet, knowing it would be a long time before I heard the sounds of Africa again.

At last I turned and walked back towards the house, my mind now pre-occupied with the prospect of my final, chilling task. Michael was standing silently by the Land Cruiser. His normally inscrutable face showed small signs of distress, his lips thin and pursed.

"Let's get Sam inside the car," I said. Michael opened the door. "Come on, Sammy, in you get." The dog, always keen for a ride, jumped in and settled himself on the back seat, thumping his tail excitedly. Cindy made to follow.

"Not you, my girl," I said, shutting the door on her nose, "you can stay with us for a bit." Cindy wagged her tail, happy to listen to my voice. Suddenly her ears cocked and she turned to face the gate, growling softly. A car was turning slowly into the driveway. I patted Cindy's head gently. "It's okay, girl. We're expecting." I didn't move, as I watched the car slowly trundle down the driveway and pull to a stop. The door opened, and a plump woman with tousled blonde hair climbed out.

"Graham?"

"Hi."

"Hi." I shook her hand.

"This is Michael." The gardener was hovering respectfully in the background.

"*Mangwanani,* Michael. *Marara ere?*" Good morning, how are you? Her tone was kindly.

Michael smiled. "*Tarara marara au.*" I am well if you are also.

"And who is this?" the woman asked, bending down to stroke the dog standing tensed next to me.

"This is Cindy. She's the smart one."

The woman stood up again. "You haven't changed your mind?"

"No. And I appreciate you coming here. It makes it easier for us."

"Under the circumstances, it's the least I can do." She was fiddling with the catch on a black bag. "I think, perhaps, over there, in the shade."

"Okay." We moved across to a patch of dappled green, Michael following us hesitantly. I sat down on the grass, Cindy snuggling up next to me. I stroked her coat. Michael stood silently a couple of metres away. Sam, still shut in the car, woofed with jealousy, wondering why his ride was being delayed.

"This must be a difficult time for you?"

"Difficult for all of us, I suppose." I wondered what to say next. "I, er... I just didn't know what to do with the dogs. Everyone's leaving. We worried they would be neglected."

The blonde woman had opened her bag. She rummaged inside, then withdrew a small bottle. As I watched, she carefully filled a syringe with yellow liquid. "You shouldn't feel bad," she soothed. "I see it every day. Horses, dogs, cats. It's worse on the farms where the farmers have been thrown out by the war vets. The ill-treatment of some of the animals would make your hair stand on end." She leaned over and patted Cindy's leg. "Okay, girl, this won't hurt." Then the vet gently inserted the needle into the dog's vein. Cindy whined and looked at me. I noticed Michael had joined us. He stroked the dog's head gently, murmuring something in Shona.

"This is never easy," continued the vet, "but given the situation, you've made the right choice."

I nodded, and turned back to my dog. Her eyes were watching me, obedient, trusting. "There, there," I murmured, "good girl."

Then the syringe was empty. I felt Cindy's muscles relax. Her brown eyes glazed over, and I couldn't stop a small tear falling to the ground.

"Sorry, baas."

Sorry. Africans use the word not as an apology, but as empathy for those in distress. It conveys understanding in the face of helplessness. With Africa's endless victims, it is a word that is in danger of getting worn out.

"Thanks, Michael." I knew he meant it. "Now you'd better get Sam."

I stood for the last time on the cool dark veranda of the house, trying to erase the memory of the last hour from my mind. As I stood there, my gaze was drawn across the garden, across the new patch of red earth where the dogs now lay at peace, to the view of the valley and the trees on the far hillside. It had been our dream to live here amongst these hills and trees, to surround ourselves in nature's shimmering red and orange.

I stepped down from the veranda and walked slowly across the lawn. Curled *msasa* pods crackled underfoot, and the scent of hibiscus floated on the air. Nature carried on its daily routine unfazed by my personal grief. A purple-crested lourie called from a tree, *Ko-ko-ko-ko*, then swooped overhead, crimson under-feathers flashing. Bees hummed busily around the flowerbeds.

I stopped at the granite-edged swimming pool, the deep blue-green water as enticing as ever. Memories of Kyle and Chelsea frolicking in the water flickered like a home movie behind my eyes. Their laughter still seemed to echo in the branches of the overhanging trees.

I walked towards the viewpoint overlooking the river, to the bench where we had so often sat, beers in hand, watching the seasons change in the valley below. Today, a warm breeze was blowing, carrying the chatter of weaver birds and red-collared widows. A buzzard circled overhead on an up-draught. Down the valley, where the farmlands were, wisps of smoke from cooking fires drifted lazily into the rinsed yellow-blue sky. How does one drink in a view that you will never see again?

A cockerel's throaty cry drifted up the hill. I thought how easy it was to be mesmerised by this apparent blanket of peace. The calmness belied the political turmoil raging in the farmlands not so far away, where hate and fire and evil held sway, could come surging up our valley at any moment.

There was a snap of a twig behind me. I turned. Michael was quietly standing there, respecting my solitude.

"Come here," I beckoned my faithful servant.

Michael came across hesitantly and stood beside me. Younger than me in years, now he looked older, more wizened, the burden of the future already weighing on his stooped shoulders. I had put money in a bank account for him, and shown him how his family could live off the interest if they were careful. But how could I tell him that I feared for his future more than I did for mine? I could catch a plane to Australia, and find a new job, and predictably survive, but none of that was possible for Michael. He and his family would have to face Zimbabwe's future at ground level, coming face to face with the gathering political storm that was sweeping across our land. What madness might engulf him? What would be the odds of his survival? I couldn't bear to contemplate it.

Side by side, victims of events too big for either of us to control, we stood together and looked down the valley into the blue haze of our shared homeland. I realised that I had been mentally ready for all the other hard goodbyes that I had had to make, but in the chaos of last minute packing, I had forgotten to brace myself to farewell my faithful servant. I didn't know what to say.

"You did a good job with this garden, Michael," I murmured, breaking the silence.

"Before. Now it is time to rest." A hint of a sigh escaped his yellowed teeth.

We stood in silence again.

"It is time for me to go," I said at last. Michael turned to look at me, his gnarled, work-worn hands clenched tightly around his tattered green cap. Tears were trickling down his face.

"Master…" He choked to a halt.

Neither of us could speak. Salt stung the back of my eyes. In an unaccustomed embrace, I clasped Michael's hands tightly. The red soil on his fingers was cool to the touch, but the roughness of his grey skin had the warm heart of Africa coursing through it. As I drew him into an awkward hug, I could smell the familiar wood smoke on his grubby work clothes. I knew his was the final embrace of a continent that had carried me in its arms, close to its soul, all my life. Now I was turning my back on the land and the people that had grown me. I was overwhelmed.

Eventually I found my voice. "Goodbye, Mhaka," I choked. *"Hamba gashle.* Go carefully."

Then I walked away.

52 Perth, January 2001

The Arrivals Hall beams with lightness - bright, air-conditioned, crisply clean. Passengers bustle across the wide concourse, their criss-crossing footsteps muffled by a spotless grey carpet. Chrome stanchions, sparkling under a winking dome of halogen lights, reflect an unfamiliar efficiency. I sense that there is an unseen organising hand behind the scenes guiding everything so that it is done just right. It's so different to the stuttering half-chaos I have left behind in Africa. I breathe deeply, inhaling the smell of polite efficiency. A smartly dressed woman in a blue uniform catches my eye, smiles. Her blonde pony-tail wags like a friendly dog's tail.

We are the last passengers in a long queue that shuffles towards the immigration desk. But I am in no hurry. I feel I need to savour every moment of this first taste of freedom, to soak it all in, to reassure myself that we are indeed rid of that scowling, angry, bitter darkness that we have left behind. Only twelve hours ago we had had to face the last hurdle, Zimbabwe customs:

"Are you carrying any Zimbabwe currency?" the surly official in threadbare jacket had glowered at me. I had almost laughed then, almost told him where he could shove his worthless Zim dollars. Instead, I simply told him I had a hundred dollars, just enough to buy one Coke before getting on the plane. Then he had waved us through, and we walked into the future.

Now, as we wait patiently in line, I look out through sparkling plate glass windows, into the shimmering heat haze that announces the start of an Australian summer. The distant landscape is washed flat beneath a cloudless dome of blue sky. The sky in Australia seems so wide, so crisply clear!

"Good day, sir." The immigration officer behind the desk motions for me to step forward. "Welcome to Perth." The official greeting is shocking in its politeness and sincerity.

I face the immigration officer, my stomach knotting itself like it always does at border posts. My memory of border crossings in Africa is of tense encounters with surly and drunk officials, a sneer on their lips as they intimidate or look for a bribe. The Australian official just smiles encouragingly at me, waiting for my passport.

Suddenly the lightness of this strange new place seems to swirl around - it rises like a wave from my feet, surging through my body, overwhelming my fragmented thoughts of the past. I feel as if a huge weight is lifting from my shoulders. I hold on to the edge of the desk as I struggle to keep my balance.

"I feel like I just escaped from jail," I whisper.

"Pardon, sir? Are you all right?"

I blink hard, until I can again see the sharpness of the wood-grain desk in front of me. I look at the immigration official. He has steady brown eyes above a well trimmed black beard, flecked with grey. Iraqi? Afghan? Pakistani, perhaps? I stare into the depths of the man's face. I want him to know how important this moment is to me. My throat catches with an inexplicable lump.

"Thank-you," I croak. "Thank-you for letting us come here." Salty tears prick behind my eyes.

The immigration officer holds my gaze for a moment, then his eyes flick away. He is no longer looking at me, he is staring far away. Immediately, instinctively I know he is remembering his own past, his own journey, a journey maybe like mine, probably worse, a ruined life smeared with torture and anguish. I stand there, silent.

Slowly the officer's eyes return to the present. He focuses back on my eyes. A smile flickers across his lips. An unspoken understanding exists between us, born of our shared fate.

"Don't worry mate," he says gently. "It'll be all right."

Epilogue

When Debby, my first serious girlfriend, dumped me (it turned out that she had found another man), my sense of devastation was total. I felt heartbreak, betrayal, rejection. She had been my first true love, and the loneliness and despair in my stomach was unbearable. Like every other jilted lover, I raged, wept, sought solace and plotted revenge. I tried to replay the past in my mind, looking for clues as to why it had happened and searching for things I could have done differently. It took me ten years to get over her, but finally I managed to accept the loss, forgive, and get on with my life.

Looking back now, I realise that from the moment my life became intertwined with hers, there was a certain historical inevitability about the course of our relationship - our personalities and our pasts were like faulty compasses that would inevitably steer us onto treacherous rocks, destroying everything, leaving only splintered memories of a happier time.

With the benefit of hindsight, I see a similar, uncanny parallel in my love affair with Africa. Seduced by Africa's beauty and charms, enervated by her rhythms and raw passion, I threw caution aside and gave her my heart. For as long as I can remember, I have been madly, totally, infatuated with her.

But again, the compass which guided us was faulty, and there were traps everywhere for the unwary. As we journeyed together, jealousy took the tiller, and greed pulled our ship off course. For me, there has been a familiar, sickening inevitability to it all. Once again, my love has foundered on the rocks of despair, the dream is destroyed, backs have turned in rejection. On Africa, the worst cynics appear to have been vindicated; in spite of her allure, she has affirmed that she is a fickle, unpredictable creature. Now crushed, bloodied, scared to death, I have simply turned tail and run.

I am in good company, for fully a third of Zimbabwe's population has fled the country's economic meltdown and Robert Mugabe's continuing oppression. Like detritus from a shipwreck, we, the survivors, wash up on foreign shores.

For those trapped in Zimbabwe, ten years after the storm began to rage, life just gets worse and worse. A new generation is growing up there knowing only hunger, violence and chaos.

From my distant bridgehead in Australia, I watch, mute and saddened at the loss and needless waste. Spurned by the homeland which I love, I do not know what to do. I cannot go back, yet I struggle to go forward. I lick my wounds, and shuffle my memories one more time around the table.

Glossary of Local Words

Agh sis!	An expression of revulsion
Agric-Alert	Security radio network set up to link remote farms
Aikona	No
AK-47	Russian made automatic rifle, the weapon of choice for guerrilla armies worldwide owing to its ease of use and reliability
Apartheid	Literally "living apart". South Africa's pre-1989 system of separate development for separate racial groups.
Babbelaas	Hangover
Bail	Fall, stop doing
Barny	Fight
B-car	Police car
Biltong	Dried jerky
Bobbejaan	Baboon
Boet, boetie	Brother, little brother
Boog	Derogatory term for a black person
Braai	Barbeque
Bundu	Bushland
Bundu-bashing	Walking or driving through the bush
Bung	Afraid
Cabin	House
Camo'	Camouflage
Casevac	Casualty evacuation
Charlie Tango, CT	Communist terrorist
Checha!	Hurry up!
Cheers	Thanks

Chef	Chief, boss
Chete	Only
China	Friend, buddy
Chips!	Watch out!
Chopper	Helicopter
Chuck	Vomit
Chuffed	pleased
Clap	Hit
Clunks	Smells bad
Commie	Communist
Crash	sleep
Cubby hole	Glove compartment
Curry muncher	Derogatory term for an Indian person
Cut	Go
Dagga	Mud. Also marijuana
DC	District Commissioner
Deck	Knock down
Dingus	Thing
Doff	Stupid
Donner	Hit
Doos	Stupid person
Dop	Drink
Doss	Sleep
Dwaal	Wander
Eina!	Ouch!
Faga moto	Hurry up. Literally "make fire"
Flatdog	Crocodile
Floppy	Derogatory term for a black person
FN	Fabrique Nationale 7.62mm rifle, standard issue for the Rhodesian armed forces
Gandanga	Terrorist
Gap, gap it, take the gap	Run, flee

Gas	A good time
Gat	Gun
Goffel	Derogatory term for a Coloured (mixed blood) person
Gondie	Derogatory term for a black person
Gook	Terrorist
Graft	Work
Graunch	Fondle, kiss
Graze	Eat (v); food (n)
Gukurahundi	Literally "the rains that wash away the dust". The name given to Mugabe's putsch against the Matabele people and armed dissidents supportive of his political rival and acclaimed "Father of Zimbabwe", Joshua Nkomo. During the early 1980's, as the world ignored growing evidence of the atrocity, Mugabe's infamous Korean-trained Fifth Brigade slaughtered an estimated 20,000 Matabele peasants
Hamba gashle	Go carefully
Handei	Let's go
Hapana	No
Hazeku indaba	No problem, no worries
Hobo	A lot
Hokoyo!	Danger, watch out!
Hondo	War
Honky	Derogatory term for a white person
Hout	Derogatory term for a black person
Howzit?	Hello
IMF	International Monetary Fund
Impi	Tribal fighting unit
In the sticks	In the bush

Indunas	Elders or senior leaders within the tribe
Int	Intelligence, information
Item	Thing. Can also refer to a girl-friend
Izzit?	Oh really?
Jack	Steal. Also zero
Jambanja	Literally "turning everything upside-down". Mugabe's orchestrated campaign using the war vets to force white farmers off the land
Jeez!	Jesus!
Jesse	Very thick thorn bush
Jigging	Having sex
Jorl	Party, joy ride
Just now	In a while - could be anywhere from a few minutes time to a couple of hours. (See also "now now")
Kaffir	Derogatory term for a black person. From the Arabic for "unbeliever"
Kak	Shit, trouble
Kay	Kilometre
Kenge	Excellent
Kia, khaya	Small house
Knobkerrie	Fighting stick
Kopje	Rocky hill, outcrop
Kraal	Group of huts, village
Laager	Defensive circle of wagons
Laaitie	Child
Lank	Long, a lot
Lekker	Good, nice
M.A.G.	Machine gun
Mai we	My word, gosh!
Mandebvu	Bearded man
Maningi	Many
Manji-manji	Now now = immediately

Marungu	White man
Mashona (Shona)	Bantu tribe that settled in the highveld areas of what is now Zimbabwe. Shona = their language
Matabele (Ndebele)	Offshoot group of the warlike Zulu tribe that settled in the south and west of what is now Zimbabwe. Ndebele = their language
Mazvita	Thank-you
Mealies	Maize, corn
Mina aikona asi	I don't know
Mombies	Cattle
Mompara	Idiot
Mopane	Type of lowveld tree
Msasa	Type of highveld tree
Mujiba	Young informant, messenger
Mukka	Friend
Munt	Derogatory term for a black person. From "muntu", people
Mushi	Good, nice
Muti	Medicine
Nail	Kill
NCO	Non-commissioned officer
Now now	Immediately
Nganga	Witchdoctor
Nut	Head
Ou, oun	Person
Owie, man!	Ouch, you!
Pamberi!	Forward!
Park off	Relax
Peg	Die
Penga	Mad
Picannin	Child

PK	Picannin kia = toilet
Plough	Fail
Poep'ol	Arsehole, a jerk
Pookie	Lightweight land-mine detecting vehicle with broad tyres. Designed by the Rhodesian security forces to clear mined roads
Poonda	Woman
Prang	Crash
Pull	Kill
Pungwe	indoctrination session attended by peasants
PV	Protected village, a fenced and guarded compound for the forced relocation of rural peasants
Rand	Unit of South African currency. 100 cents = 1 Rand
RDR	Rhodesia Defence Regiment, unit comprising Coloured troops
Rev	Attack, shoot up
Rhodie	Rhodesian
Rinderpest	A severe disease of cattle and hoofed game which leads to widespread animal deaths
RLI	Rhodesian Light Infantry. Elite paratroop and assault unit
Rock spider	Derogatory term for an Afrikaans person
Rock up	Arrive
RPG	Rocket propelled grenade
RTU	Returned to unit. Underperforming officer cadets would be demoted and returned to basic troop training in Bulawayo

Safe, ek se	Cool, man
Scale	Steal
Scheme	Plot, plan, tell
Settler	Revolutionary term for white farmer
Shamwari	Friend
Shateen	Bushland
Shebeen	Informal drinking place
Shupa	trouble, upset
Skellum; skebanga	Pest, bad person
Skinner	Talk behind someone's back
Skrik	Fright
Slot	Shoot, kill
Smaak	Like, have a crush on
Spoor	Animal tracks
Square	Sorted out, fair, debt paid
Ster	Sister
Sterek	Sure, strong
Stingers	Schoolyard game involving throwing a tennis ball at each other
Stir	Cause trouble
Stoked	Pleased
Stop street	Stop sign
Stroppy	Cheeky, argumentative
Struze bob	It's true
Sut	No
Taken out	Killed
Takkies	Tennis shoes
Tatenda	Thank-you very much
Terr	Terrorist
The moer in	Annoyed
Tokolosh	Evil spirit
Tune me	Tell me

UDI	Unilateral Declaration of Independence by Rhodesia from Britain in 1965
Umfazi	Woman
Varsity	University
Vasbyt	Stand fast
Veld	Bushland
Veldskoene	Bush shoes
Vlei	Low-lying waterlogged grassland
Voetsak	Bugger off, go away
Vrek (frek)	Die
War vets, wovits	War veterans (but also used as a generic term to include all hangers-on who joined in the free-for-all land grab on white commercial farms)
White phos	White phosphorous, napalm
Whitey	Derogatory term for a white person
Woos	Softie, weakling
Yah, ja	Yes
ZANLA	Zimbabwe National Liberation Army (Mugabe's forces)
ZANU-PF	Mugabe's political party
ZAPU	Nkomo's political party
Zim, Zimbo	Zimbabwe, Zimbabwean
ZIPRA	Zimbabwe Peoples Revolutionary Army (Nkomo's forces)
Zol	Marijuana cigarette
Zot	Derogatory term for a black person

Printed in Great Britain
by Amazon